Timeless Digital Marketing

Ahmad Abugosh

Timeless Digital Marketing

Ahmad Abugosh

Leanpub

This is a Leanpub book. Leanpub empowers authors and publishers with the Lean Publishing process. Lean Publishing is the act of publishing an in-progress ebook using lightweight tools and many iterations to get reader feedback, pivot until you have the right book and build traction once you do.

© 2019 Ahmad Abugosh

Contents

About The Author 1

Introduction 3

Chapter 1 - Why Digital Marketing? 5
    Traditional Marketing 6
    Digital / Online Marketing 8

Chapter 2 - The Channels 11
    Digital - Push Marketing 12
    Digital - Pull Marketing 26
    Digital - Long Term Marketing 38
    Digital - Retention Marketing 40
    Channel Conclusion 45

Chapter 3: Setting your foundations 47
    Tracking Traffic 47
    Tracking Conversions 50
    Performance Goals 51
    Awareness Goals 52
    Focusing On Performance Goals 55
    Tracking Performance Goals 56
    Ad Platform Pixels 60
    Tag Managers 61
    Tracking B2B versus B2C 63

CONTENTS

Chapter 4 - How to NOT waste money! 67
    Budgets 67
    You may already have a budget 68
    You don't have a budget 68
    Planning Your Strategy 75

Chapter 5 - Getting Immediate Results 79
    Creating Paid Campaigns 79
    Targeting- Starting with a Niche 80
    How to reach them 85
    Pull Marketing 97

Chapter 6 - Getting Free Traffic 103
    Long Term Marketing Strategy 103
    Search Engine Optimization (SEO) 104
    Organic Social Media 123
    Email Newsletters 128

Chapter 7 - Measuring results 147
    The Digital Ad Funnel 147
    1 - Conversion Rate 149
    2- CPA (Cost per acquisition) 151
    3- Revenue, Margins and Profit 152
    Action Plan 166

Chapter 8 - What do you do if it's working? 169
    Bringing down our CPA 169
    Playing with your levers to find the optimal level 170
    Beware of the budget plateau 171
    Action Plan 173

Chapter 9 - What to do if it's not working? 175
    Change the targeting 176
    Change the ads 180
    Adjust the bids / budgets 181
    Softer conversions 182

Change the landing page	182
Change the price	185
Change the product	186

Chapter 10 - Strategies for Growth 187
    Strategy 1 Long term CLV 187
    Strategy 2: The 20% approach 191
    Strategy 3: The Inbound Approach 193
    Strategy 4: The Hybrid Approach 198

Conclusion - Now what do I do? 201

Glossary of terms 205

Appendix of Tools 215

About The Author

Ahmad Abugosh has been working full-time in Digital Marketing since 2012. He is the current Director of Marketing & Learning Programs at AstroLabs, where he handles all marketing, running of academy programs and tech systems at AstroLabs. Ahmad graduated with a degree in Computer Engineering from the American University of Sharjah in 2011, and has been Google Certified (in Analytics & Google Ads) since 2012. Since then, he has worked at MBC, Namshi (Rocket Internet) and a digital agency in Dubai (RBBi, where he worked on Analytics and BI setups for some of the largest organizations in the region). His professional expertise is in Analytics, Digital Marketing, Fullstack Web Development and Tech Workshops.

This book is the culmination of his more than 7 years of experience working in the digital marketing field and training thousands of people through in-person workshops and online courses.

You can connect with Ahmad on:

LinkedIn: https://linkedin.com/in/ahmadabugosh/

Twitter: https://twitter.com/aabugosh

Personal Website: https://ahmadabugosh.com

Email: ahmadabugosh@gmail.com

Introduction

If you had told me when I first graduated from university that I would be working in marketing, I would have laughed. Now, here I am 8 years later writing a book on marketing. How did this happen?

As someone that is technically minded (I made my first website when I was only 10 years old back in 1998), I was always into computers, the internet, and programming, but never understood marketing. I used to listen to the late Bill Hicks' comedy sketch on marketing and laugh along at how inept and soulless marketing was as a profession. I studied Computer Engineering partly because of how much I loved computers and partially because of how much I disliked what I perceived as sleazy business and sales. One thing changed though since then, I got a job.

I started working as a web developer straight out of college. I initially really liked the job, but I found working on a large code base not very demanding. (In hindsight, I would have probably loved the field if the company and nature of the work was different.) That's why when I saw an online ad for an eCommerce company looking to hire, I immediately applied to an entry level marketing position. I was more excited about the eCommerce part than the fact that it was a marketing role, since I was thinking that it would be cool to see how an eCommerce company is run. Little did I know that that one choice would lead me on a trajectory to getting immersed in digital marketing that would change my life forever, and without that one late evening decision, I think it's safe to say this book wouldn't exist.

After working in that eCommerce company for a couple of years, I learned a ton about digital marketing from some of the brightest people I ever came across. After that, I moved on to work at an agency helping other companies implement the digital marketing best practices I learned. I now teach and mentor companies and individuals at a company called AstroLabs located in Dubai, UAE and have shared what I learned in workshops and learning sessions with over 1,000 people (at the time of writing this book.)

My goal is for this book is to extend that knowledge to you and to teach you the fundamental strategies and techniques I learned (without getting into the weeds of too many details right away) so you can walk away with a practical roadmap to a **timeless** understanding of Digital Marketing.

"Wait a minute," you might think. Digital Marketing is one of the most evolving fields in the world. Almost every day you hear about new changes to platforms, new companies, and new targeting strategies. What exactly is "timeless" about that? Well, my friend, that's exactly the point of this book. Since Digital Marketing is such a constantly changing field, you're right, it is often hard to keep up. However, there are many things in Digital Marketing that do not change. These fundamental principles have been around for the last 10+ years, and they will most likely be around for decades more. Will the way you use these principles change? Of course. However, as long as you understand how these timeless strategies work, you'll have a very strong base of understanding when it comes to Digital Marketing, which will allow you to always stay up to date, no matter how fast the industry changes.

Don't be confused and think that this book is theoretical though. It is packed with practical exercises and action plans for you to follow (at the end of every chapter, as well as at the end of the book), and by the time you get through this book you will live the **Timeless Digital Marketing** principles, and truly be able to market any business!

Chapter 1 - Why Digital Marketing?

Before we can get into Digital Marketing, let's talk about marketing in general, since I often feel like a lot of people have a negative opinion on it, and feel it's a sleazy profession.

Let's first define marketing. Marketing is the way in which you promote something (usually a product or a service). That's it. I think marketing can be a very manipulative and disingenuous field, but it's something that we as humans have to do in every aspect of our lives. If you zoom out even more, it's about persuasion and convincing people that you can help them improve their lives, and it's something we all do on a daily basis. For example, if you want to have your friend go out with you somewhere you have to persuade them of your plan (or market the idea to them), in order to convince them. It's not manipulative, as long as your intentions aren't manipulative, and you have the other person's best interests at heart. Ok, so you might be saying, this got into the weeds really quickly, why are we talking about persuasion, I want a practical guide for my business? You're right, but it's important to establish a common language of understanding to start.

What is marketing? Marketing is the process by which you promote goods and services. That's the textbook definition, but for me, I believe that marketing is showing people the value of what you can offer to help them improve their lives.

Marketing can take many forms. What I want to cover in the next section is what are the main types of marketing, to set the context into our wider discussion before we get into digital marketing.

Traditional Marketing

Before I get into digital marketing, let me first talk about how marketing worked in the pre-digital age (in other words: the age before the internet). Before computers and the internet, how could you get the word out about something you were selling? You had four main ways.

Push Marketing

The first way was to "push" your ad in front of others. This is also often what people refer to as advertising, since you are actively promoting what your product or service (most likely by paying for the privilege). This could be by buying a billboard ad, tv, or radio commercial, or by distributing a flyer. The problem with this way is that you had to incur a lot of cost to get the word out, without knowing exactly what worked and what didn't. There is a saying attributed to John Wanamaker which states, "Half the money I spend on advertising is wasted; the trouble is I don't know which half." That was the problem in this type of "push" marketing.

Pull Marketing

The second way that you could traditionally market your business was to hope that people come to you (by convenience of your location, or a listing somewhere). This form of marketing is often called "pull" marketing, because you are pulling in people to your business, as opposed to pushing your ad out to them. You don't just have to wait around though, there are active ways for you to get people to come to you. For example, you could list your business in a directory (like the yellow pages, or through local business listings), and wait for people to contact you. What you should keep in mind though, is that this form of marketing generally is one that has less volume (since you are only in contact with people that are already looking for you or your service); however, on the flip side, it's a way of marketing that generally has a lot more *qualified* interest. In other words, the people that come to you are generally a lot more interested in your product or service than a random person who may see an ad.

Long-Term Marketing

The third type of marketing relates to building consistent growth over time. This includes building your brand to an extent that people know about you (also known as branding), and growing through sustainable long-term efforts, like building trust, word of mouth, attending trade shows, community events etc. There are no shortcuts here— it's all about building trust and focusing on long term gains and efforts.

Retention & Loyalty

The fourth and final main way to market to people is not really to market to anyone new at all, but just to keep serving people that already know about you. This is often a good strategy because it is far less expensive to keep a current customer than to get a new customer. (Conservative estimates are that it is 5 times cheaper.) So, oftentimes, if a business has enough customers in the door, all they have to do is keep them coming back to stay in business. Think about the local corner grocery store. They probably don't have to do much marketing because they have people coming in that already know about them, are loyal, and consistently purchase their weekly supplies there. Of course, this requires some initial marketing to build the initial pool of customers, but once a business establishes a base of loyal customers, it can be sustainable just to focus on retaining them.

Digital / Online Marketing

Now let's switch back to the digital world. First of all, let's define what digital marketing is. Digital marketing is basically marketing done through digital means, which in a practical sense means any marketing that is done over the internet or online. That is why people often use digital marketing and online marketing interchangeably.

So, what makes digital marketing different and by most accounts a much more effective way to do marketing than traditional offline marketing? It has to do with the nature of the platform, which can take advantage of the following levers:

1. **You can track everything.** This is the most important factor that gives digital marketing an immense advantage over other forms of marketing. You can measure exactly who sees, engages, clicks, contacts, and buys online so you know exactly what marketing efforts had a positive effect on your business. Going back to the quote "Half the money I spend on advertising (marketing) is wasted"...while that may have been true for traditional marketing, with digital marketing, it is not the case. Nearly everything can be tracked, and you can know what money you spend is working and what is not.

2. **You can start now.** You don't need 1000's of dollars in capital upfront to launch an online campaign. Many of the techniques in this book are 100% free; even the ones that are paid, don't require large investments, since for most businesses you can set things up in a way where you make back what you spend so you don't need a large amount of capital.

3. **You can target anyone.** You are not tied down like you are in offline marketing. You can be in India and market to people in Mexico. You can also be super-specific, like only show ads to moms interested in home cooking that recently moved houses (I'll explain how to do that later in the book).

4. **You can easily make changes.** You are agile! With digital marketing, it is completely up to you whether you start or stop a campaign. If something is not working, you can immediately turn it off. If something is working, you can scale it up. You have complete control.

5. **You get a better ROI (Return on Investment).** As a result of all the reasons above, digital marketing has a much better ROI compared to traditional marketing. From a business standpoint, this is perfect, as it allows you to know the direct return on everything that you spend. For example, if you spend $1 on marketing, you can know that it brought you $10 in revenue. As a result, you can easily project your revenue and costs in a much more efficient manner.

Chapter 2 - The Channels

Before we get into specific recommendations and how to implement each channel, let's first make sure that we understand the main areas that we can work with in digital marketing. There will always be new channels and strategies within these areas, but you will find that all digital marketing has to fall under one of them main categories, which are similar to the four categories outlined in the first chapter.

The four main categories or types of channels are the same as the ones for traditional marketing, but there are important differences with each of them that make digital marketing more effective as a strategy.

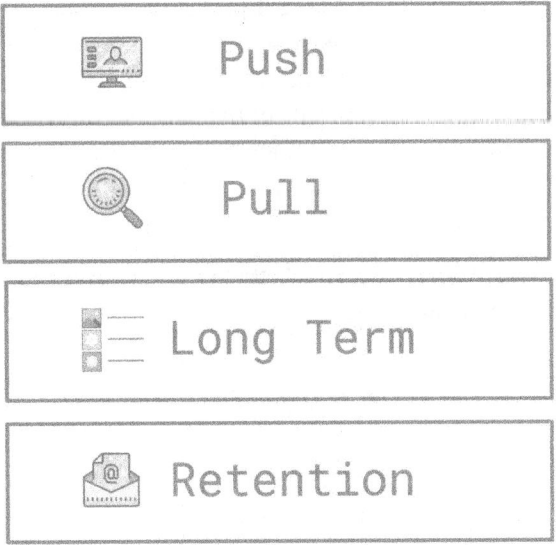

The 4 Channel Types

Digital - Push Marketing

The act of paying to push your ad to people while they are living their lives (or browsing online). Some people call this *interruption marketing* or *permissionless marketing*. This is what people typically think about when they hear the word "marketing."

Before the internet, push marketing consisted of all ads on TV, Radio, Billboards, and anyone else where consumers were shown images and videos. However, what's different nowadays is everything can be tracked. This is where you show your ads to people while they're doing something else. Basically, you interrupt them while they're trying to just live their life. In the context of digital marketing, this is showing people ads while they are **browsing** online. The format of these ads is usually either images or videos and are usually called **display ads**. Let me give an example of this. Let's say that Sarah is watching YouTube videos. If she's on YouTube for about an hour, she'll probably see dozens of display ads (as long as she doesn't have an ad blocker enabled). She would see image banner ads that would appear on top of the page, overlays on top of videos, and on the side of the page next to videos, as well as video ads which may appear before a video starts (some of which she can skip and some she can't) or at any point during the videos she's watching.

There are a few types of channels that fall under push marketing or these kinds of display ads.

Ad Networks

These are marketplaces that allow advertisers to connect with content creators through a third-party platform. For example, if Zak has a blog that is getting a lot of visitors, he may want to start making money on his blog by showing ads to users. The problem is, how can he find advertisers that would be willing to pay him for showing their ads on his website? He could go about finding them on his own (which would be very time consuming if he is just starting out), or he could join an ad network. By installing a piece of code on his site, he'll be able to join an ad network immediately which will automatically connect him with advertisers willing to pay to show their image or video ad on his website, which will allow him to start making money from his blog from day 1.

```
            Advertisers
            Create Ads
```

```
┌─────────────────────────────────────┐
│            Ad Network               │
│  Marketplace Aggregator for Ads     │
└─────────────────────────────────────┘
```

```
         Ads are displayed
         Content Creators
```

Ad Networks

The largest example of this is the **Google Display Network** (which is so large that 90% of internet users on a daily basis, see at least one Google Display Network ad). From the advertiser side, (which is the focus of this book) **Google Ads** (formerly known as Google AdWords) is the platform used and from the content creator side (where the ad is shown), **AdSense** is used. (On average. Google takes a 40% cut of what the advertiser pays, while giving the other 60% to the content creator.)

Targeting

As an advertiser, you have a few options to choose from when it comes to who sees your ads. You could either choose to target the **content** (website or app) that serves the ad (the content or **context** of the ad), or you could target the **user**, which targets them based on their **browsing behavior** (what websites or apps they visited in the past).

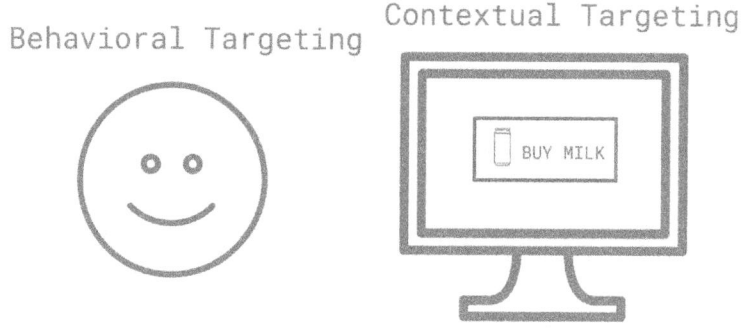

Targeting

Ads on the Google Display Network are usually targeted in a **contextual** way, which means that advertisers target the content itself (the topic of the content), and not the demographics or behavior of the people consuming the content. However, you can still target users in a **behavioral** way by showing ads to people based on their browsing behavior. For example, that's why it's possible to see an ad for a laptop on a gardening website. If the advertiser selling the laptop targeted "gardening" websites, that would be contextual targeting. What's more likely though is that the advertiser targeted people "interested in" (previously looked at) laptops online, so the ad will be served to them regardless of how irrelevant the website they are on is.

Paid Social Media

The second major push channel that started becoming popular from around the time Facebook took off (in 2007) is paid social media ads. Since the growth of websites like Facebook, Instagram, Snapchat, Twitter, Pinterest, and LinkedIn became home to where people spend a large chunk of their day, and since those platforms are free (for the most part), social media ads have really picked up, because that is where people are spending their time. What makes paid social media unique (brilliant according to some, and evil according to others), is the fact that you can show ads to users on a very specific level based on information that is gathered on the social platforms that users enter about themselves. These include things like interests of the users, user demographic data, and behaviour on the social platform itself and even other websites (more about that later). This is known as **behavioral** targeting, since as opposed to contextual targeting, you are not targeting the content of what the user is consuming (the topic of the article, video etc.), but instead you are targeting the behavior of the users themselves.

Paid Social Media Channels

Not to be confused with normal social media posting (also known as non-paid or "organic" social media), paid social media consists mainly of running ads on social media business accounts for the purpose of promoting your product or service. This section of the book is probably the one that has the potential to get outdated the quickest (because of the ever-changing nature of these platforms). Nonetheless, the main social media channels (at the time of writing this book) are:

Facebook: The major player of the last decade has been Facebook, which famously also bought Instagram in 2012 and Whatsapp in 2014. In the push marketing ads space, Facebook is by far the largest social media platform that serves ads, and if you start running ads on your own, you'll quickly notice that it is by far the most advanced in terms of its targeting and capabilities (all of the other social media platforms regularly copy its ad platform features).

Twitter: A micro-blogging platform (a place to share short SMS style updates). Ads on Twitter are usually in the form of promoted tweets.

Snapchat: Popular among younger demographics, with the ability to share "Stories" (images and videos that disappear after 24 hours).

LinkedIn: The network mainly used by professionals for business related activities and recruitment. LinkedIn has its own ad platform (where users see ads similar to the Facebook model), in addition to other paid LinkedIn services for business (like the ability to send InMail).

There are other platforms that are more niche (such as Pinterest, VK in Russia etc.), but the above are the ones that are currently the most popular with regards to international marketing globally.

The Bulk of Push Marketing Ads

We'll talk about specifics a bit later, but by combining Google Display Network ads with Paid Social Media ads, you can cover nearly all ads on the internet, since they both let you target contextually (based on the content), and behaviorally (based on the users).

So, if you follow the 80/20 principle, and want to know the most high leverage effective channels to focus on for paid ads, to start, for running digital push marketing ads, I would spend the majority of my effort targeting GDN and Paid social media ads (particularly on Facebook / Instagram).

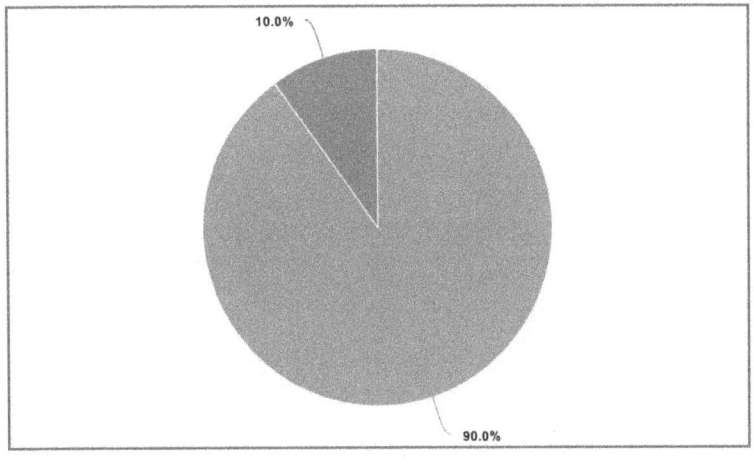

Majority of Display

That means that for the time being, if you focus all of your effort on just Google & Facebook ads, you'll get 90% of the gains of using Push marketing ads. This may change in the future, but this was the case in the digital marketing world for the last decade.

Ad Auctions

Let's say that you want to run paid Push marketing ads. How exactly do they work? In short, most ads online are served through some kind of an **online bid auction**

Let's give a simple example and say that there are two people that want to show their ads on the same channel. If they are both targeting the same user (through either contextual or behavioral targeting), they will enter an auction. The person with the highest bid wins.

Bidding Auction

How ads are displayed

When an ad is displayed to a user online, there are four actions that could take place. They are outlined in the below funnel. It is visualized as a funnel because at every stage, the number of users that take the next action drop off.

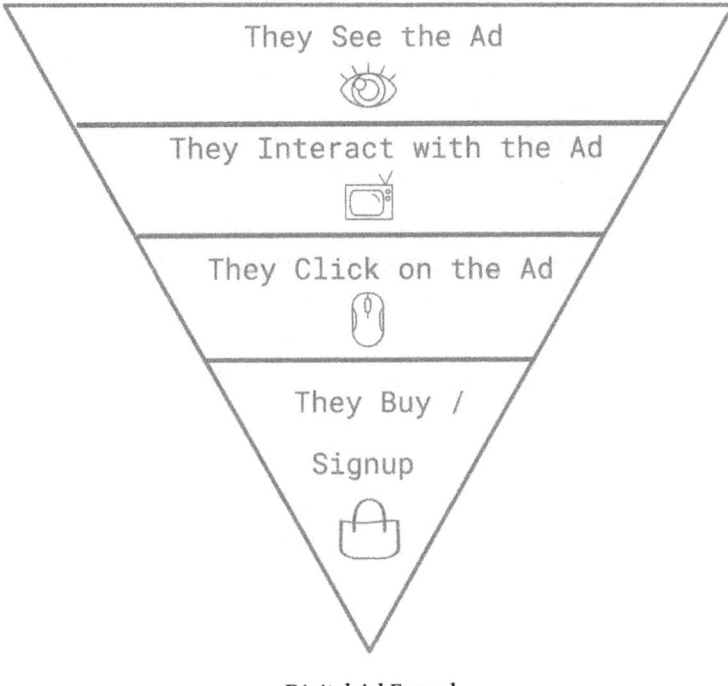

Digital Ad Funnel

They see the ad: This is also known as an **impression**. An impression means that your ad has been seen by the user, or more specifically that the ad was on the page somewhere when the page loaded for the user (if you want to know if the user had the ad in their window view, that is called a **viewable impression**). Impressions are the lowest level of tracking your ad. Impressions are mainly used to track awareness around your digital campaigns.

They interact with the ad Once they see an ad in certain formats a user can interact with it in some way without leaving the current page they're on. This could be watching a video or engaging with your ad in some way (like leaving a comment for example).

They click on the ad: The next level of digital activity online are clicks. Clicks mean that a user clicked on an ad and were directed to either a website or an app. Usually clicks should be exactly the same as website visits (also known as website sessions), however sometimes they may be slightly different (since a click is measured as soon as a user clicks on an ad, but a visit is calculated a little after the page loads, so if someone clicks on an ad, but closes the browser right away, it may count that as a click, but not as a visit).

They buy a product/ or signup: The last and final level of digital activity you'll see when running digital ads is a conversion. This is the final goal of your campaign and what denotes success. A conversion can also be referred to as a transaction or a goal. This is the last step that a user can take on your website / app.

The above levels by which users interact with ads is known as the **Digital Ad Funnel**.

Types of Bids

When it comes to how advertisers pay for ads in a bidding auction, there are 4 levels that they could bid at (based on the four areas of the Digital Ad funnel mentioned above).

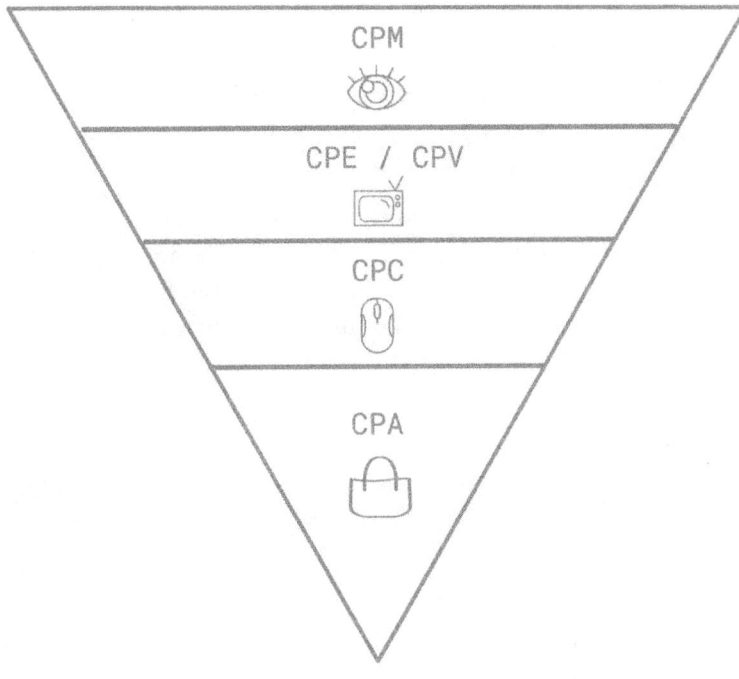

Types of Bids

CPM: Cost per milli or Cost per thousand impressions. This is where you bid on ads on an impression level (users seeing the ad). The way it is priced is based on 1,000 impressions (regardless of clicks or engagement). For example, if your CPM is $50, then you are paying $50 to get 1,000 impressions (people who see your ad). If you want to guarantee that the user actually has the ad visible in their window (and on the bottom of the page for example, some ad platforms let you bid on a "viewable impression" basis (which means that you're guaranteed that a user will at least have the ad in their browser window).

CPV Cost per video view. The amount that you pay whenever a video view is recorded. This is calculated differently on every platform. Most commonly you may come across this when you see a "skippable" ad online. A view only counts if you don't skip, watch more than 30 seconds or click on the link in the video, otherwise you don't pay anything.

CPE Cost per engagement. The amount you pay for some engagement with your ad (could be a comment, hover etc.). This method is not very commonly used online.

CPC: Cost per click. This bidding method relies on you getting a click. If a user doesn't click, then you don't pay. The amount charged is based directly on the amount of clicks you get. Since it is very performance driven, it is currently the most popular way of bidding for ads online.

CPA: Cost per acquisition. The amount you'll be expected to pay, to receive an acquisition (this is a goal that you define). If you are selling something online, you can define the amount you're willing to pay per sale as your target. For example, if you're selling a T-shirt, and for every sale you're willing to spend $10 on marketing, then your CPA can be $10.

Although CPA might seem like a lucrative option (since you'll never spend more than the amount you specify per sale), in order to turn on CPA, you have to first gather data, in order for the ad platform to activate this option, since it can only activate this option if it is something achievable. Usually this means you need to get dozens of orders per month, before it can calculate the average amount needed to market each order (your CPA).

How bids compete

So now that you know the types of bids that are available, remember that a bid means that you enter an auction with other people. So, whether or not your ad shows up, depends on if you outbid the other people in the auction.

Advertiser A	Bids $1 CPC	Wins the auction
Advertiser B	Bids $0.5 CPC	Loses the auction

Ad Auction

Bidding Amount versus Actual Amount

It's important to remember that the amount you pay in an auction is not necessarily the same as your bid amount. That is because the actual amount you pay relies mainly on the amount needed to keep your position in the auction (most platforms have this relative to 2 decimal points), while your bid amount is the maximum that you're willing to pay in the auction. For example, Advertiser A is bidding $1 CPC, they only need to pay enough to beat the next highest bid in the auction. So, if Advertiser B is bidding $0.5 CPC, then the actual amount they pay will only be $0.51.

Advertiser A	Bids $1 CPC	Wins the auction	Actual pays $0.51
Advertiser B	Bids $0.5 CPC	Loses the auction	Actual pays $0.5 (for second position)

Ad Auction Bid Amount

Different Bidding Types

But what if advertisers are bidding with different bidding types? For example, what if you are bidding on a CPC basis and I am bidding on a CPM basis? How does the bid auction compare apples and oranges?

Behind the scene it has its own conversion method. The way it works is that bids are compared on the lowest level, which is the impression level. For example, if you are bidding on a $10 CPC and I am bidding on a $50 CPM, behind the scenes the ad platform will convert your CPC bid into a CPM bid and compare it to mine. This is not seen by you but is calculated automatically by the algorithm for comparison purposes. That way you can bid CPA, CPV, CPC or CPM and compete against any other bid in the auction (without even realizing the difference).

Now that you have a basic understanding of how ad auctions work, let's get back into the other types of display ads.

Other Display Ads

Although GDN and Paid Social media account for most of the display ads served online, there are a few other types of Push Ads you should be aware of.

Other Ad Networks

The Google Display Network has definitely been the largest ad network over the last decade, however they are not the only game in town. There are other players that are trying to gain market share on this lucrative space. At the time of writing this book, the main competitor of the GDN is the Facebook Audience Network (Facebook's own ad network, that works alongside their paid social media ads, but serves ads on other non-Facebook website). It is estimated that this currently accounts for roughly 20% of the ads served through Facebook. There are also other non-Google, non-Facebook companies in the ad network space, the largest of which is Taboola and Outbrain (which in 2019 merged together as one, making it estimated to be the 3 largest ad network by size after Google and Facebook).

3rd Party Ads

These are ads that are served on websites that are not part of social media or ad networks. They account for roughly 10% of ads served online. Let me give an example. Let's say that CNN wants to show ads on their site. They could join an ad network, like the Google Display Network (GDN). However, if they do join the GDN, Google would take a cut (on average approximately 40% of the revenue they could make) from the ads they serve. Now because CNN is already a popular destination, they don't really have to rely on an ad network, because people already know about them, and advertisers could just come to them directly (like a traditional newspaper for example). You'll usually know if a website has this type of ad, because in the footer of the website, they'll have something that might say "Contact us to advertise". These types of ads may be served directly from the website that is advertising them (for example, through CDN), or they may use some kind of intermediary service like **DoubleClick** to serve the ads.

Programmatic ads

Usually run through an agency at a premium (which makes them more expensive than normal display ads), these are display ads that are served automatically and allow you to show your ads simultaneously across multiple ad networks and paid social media sites at the same time. They also allow you to integrate with 3rd party data (like census data, salary information, and other private demographic data) to allow you to run a unified campaign. Programmatic ads are usually reserved for companies with large budgets (usually more than $20,000 a month). Although they are expensive, they can be a good option for those that want to have a unified campaign across multiple channels.

Native Ads

These are promoted content pieces that are written by the website to advertise something, for example Microsoft could hire Buzzfeed to write an article like "Top ten things that you love about Windows". Although this seems like a normal post, more often than not, these are just a more sophisticated form of an ad known as **Native** advertising.

Influencer marketing

This is a marketing channel that has been on the rise, since the advent of social media channels. It basically involves having a person with a lot of followers (known as an influencer) push your message out to their followers. This can usually be done in exchange for paying them, giving them free merchandise, or using an affiliate program.

Affiliate marketing

This channel involves working with others to promote your product to their network. What's great about this channel, is that you usually don't have to pay any money to get started and sales work on a commission basis, so you only have to pay the affiliates that are promoting your product or service, if someone actually ends up buying. This arrangement usually works on a CPA (cost per acquisition) model, which means that you set a rate for a payout and if they get a customer, you pay them that amount. For example, if a company says their CPA is $50, that means that you as an affiliate will get $50 for every customer you refer. This is subject to their conditions of what they define a customer as, which could be someone paying them, or just getting someone as a lead. We'll discuss pricing models for ads in more detail in Chapter 5.

Digital - Pull Marketing

This is where you show your ad to people that are already looking for either you, or a product or service you offer. You're basically meeting people halfway. It's not pure advertising like push marketing, because you wait for people to search for something first, then you show them an ad based on what they searched for. The main channel that falls under this are Search Ads.

For most places in the world the most popular search engine has been Google for quite some time (with the only major exceptions being Yandex in Russia and Baidu in China). We'll mainly be discussing Google in this book (since it has more than 80% market share across the world), however the same principles discussed in this book can be applied to all of Google's competitors (Yahoo, Bing, Baidu, Yandex, and DuckDuckGo). With regards to Google, under this channel, the two main types of ads are **Google Search Ads** and **Google Shopping Ads**.

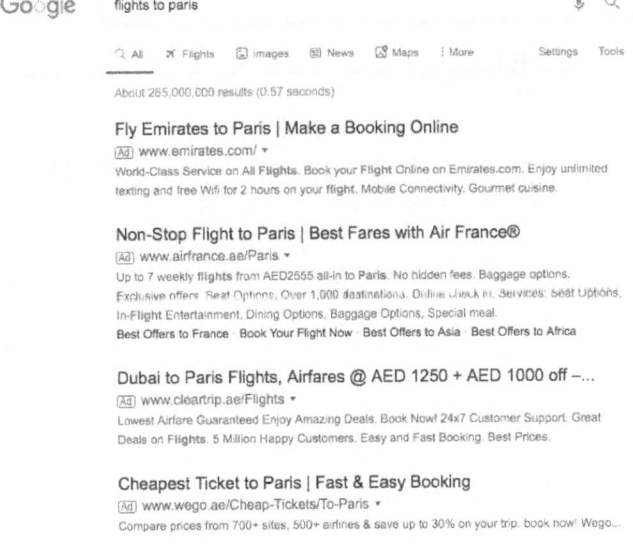

Google Search

Google Search ads are ads that appear as text ads (such as in the picture above), while Google shopping ads are ads that are tied to an eCommerce store which update based on a product feed (a list you integrate to automatically list your products).

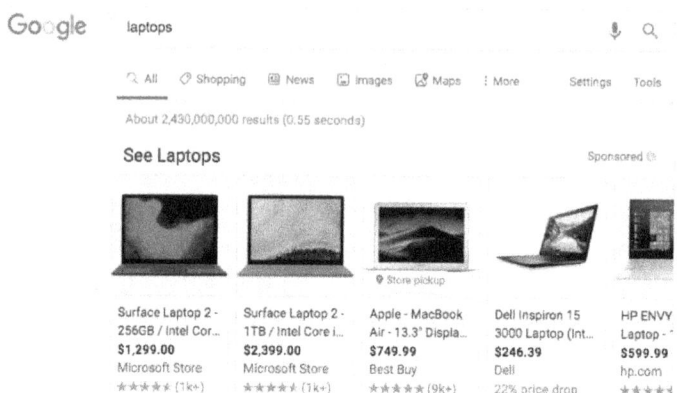

Google Shopping

Search ads are straightforward when you show ads based on keywords that are directly related to your business, but the trick is that often times people aren't directly searching for what you offer. Therefore, you may need to get creative, and think of terms people that would be interested in your product or service would search for. Let's say that you sell laptops and want to advertise them through Search Ads. If Adam is searching for a new laptop, or for a brand name of a laptop you stock, you could show him search ads directing him to learn more about what you offer. However, you could also get creative if Adam is searching for tangential terms that would indicate he's interested in a new laptop. For example, you could show your ad if he's searching for "cracked laptop screens" or "minimum specifications for software x". That won't guarantee that Adam would be interested in purchasing from seeing your ad, but it's something that a good marketer could test. Any paid listing site also falls under pull marketing. For example, any "yellow pages" type website or niche websites focused on services people can search for (for example, real estate websites, listing websites etc.).

Keywords

This form of marketing is **keyword** based, which means that the way that people find you is by choosing to show your ad to users searching for a certain word or phrase. It is a form of **contextual targeting**, because the ad you are showing depends on the keyword the user searches on the search engine, which needs to match the keyword you're targeting.

Choosing keywords

The first step to running a search ad is to figure out what are the keywords you want to target. This involves looking at:

1. Relevancy: Which is how relevant are the keywords you want to target
2. Search Volume: Which is how often people are searching for that keyword
3. Competition: Who are the people / advertisers that are also targeting that keyword
4. Price: How much should you be expected to pay to show your ad for that keyword (usually done on a CPC basis)

Keyword Types

There are several ways that you can target the same word when conducting search ads. Each way that you target a word will change the amount of times your ad will appear on searches. The 4 main ways that you can target keywords are:

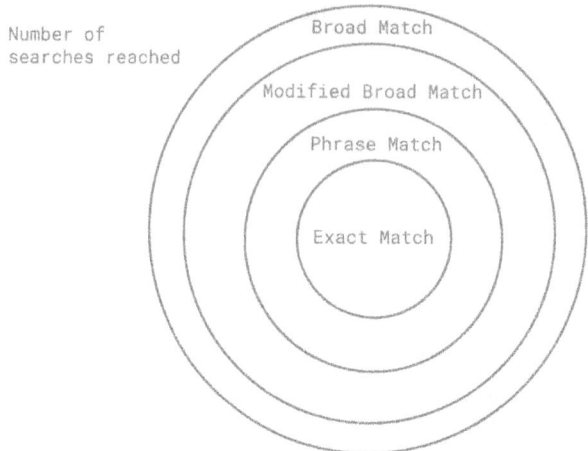

Keyword Match Types

Broad Match Will match the category of the keyword you're targeting along with its synonyms. For example, if you insert the word *cheese pizza* in your campaign, and choose **broad match**, it will show the ad for anyone searching for the word *cheese pizza* and any of its variations including any place that word is in a longer sentence.

Best cheese pizza places

pizza games

how to make a great cheese pizza

cheese calzone recipes

Etc.

As long as the word *pizza* or *cheese* is in the search, it could potentially show your ad when someone searches for that word if Google deems it as relevant. You might even notice that it shows your ad to searches with similar words (synonyms), like the last example (Calzone recipes). If you don't specify your match type, by default most search engines will target your keyword with broad match, since that will yield the highest number of searches and will cause you to spend more (even though a lot of the searches will not be relevant)

Modified Broad Match (+)

The next type of keyword type you can target is known as Modified broad match (or broad match modified). This match type is similar to broad match in that it will show your ad to all searches that contain a certain word, but the main difference is that it will not include synonyms, which makes it a little more specific. So, for example, if you target the words *cheese pizza* as a modified broad match word, it will show your ad for searches such as:

- *best cheese pizza places*
- *cheese pizza games*
- *how to make a great cheese pizza*

It will not show it, however, for searches where any of the words are exchanged for words of similar meaning. In order to make a word be a modified broad match word in Google search, you need to add a "+" to the beginning of each word you're targeting (e.g., if we want *pizza* to follow this rule, we define the keyword to be *+pizza). *

Phrase Match ("")

If you want to start getting more targeted with where your ad shows up, you can instead choose a more targeted keyword type such as **phrase match**. Phrase match will show your ad, only if that exact phrase of keyword is in the search conducted by the user. To give a clear example, let's say that you're targeting the 2-word keyword *cheese pizza*.

Your ad will show up if a user searches for:

- Cheese pizza
- Best cheese pizza
- Cheese pizza recipes

But not for:

- Cheese homemade pizza
- Pizza made of cheese
- Pizza cheese

Why? Because the phrase *cheese pizza* has to be there in the same order. If you change the order of the words, it will not show your ad, but as long as those words are in the same order (even if you add words to the beginning or end of the search), it will still show your ad.

In order to make a word be a phrase match word in Google search, you need to add double quotes, surrounding the words you're targeting. (So, if we want to target the phrase *cheese pizza* to follow this rule, we define the keyword to be *"cheese pizza".) *

Exact Match ([])

We saved the easiest for last. **Exact match** is the match type in which you target only the word you define. For example, if I target *cheese pizza *as an exact match, my ad will only show up if the user searches for exactly *cheese pizza. *

In order to make a word be an exact match word in Google search, you need to add square brackets surrounding the words you're targeting (so if we want to target the phrase *cheese pizza* to follow this rule, we define the keyword to be *[cheese pizza]). *

The only other words that may also show up are very slight misspellings a user might make. For example, if you spell the word as *cheese pizza* or make it plural like *cheese pizzas*

Example of match types versus searches they trigger

Broad Match cheese *pizza*	Modified Broad Match +cheese +pizza	Phrase Match "cheese pizza"	Exact Match [cheese pizza]
cheese pizza	cheese pizza	cheese pizza	cheese pizza
best cheese pizza	best cheese pizza	best cheese pizza	
cheese pizza near me	cheese pizza near me	cheese pizza near me	
pizza cheese store	pizza cheese store		
cheese calzone			

Match Type Example

Negative keywords (-)

Now there is another type of key you can add to your campaigns, that's not a normal keyword. **Negative** keywords are keywords you can add to your campaign, that have the purpose of preventing searches from triggering your ads if you view them as non-relevant.

For example, if there is a famous pizza game that user might search for, if you target *pizza* as a broad match keyword, someone searching for *pizza game* might see your ad. If you're a restaurant, that obviously is not someone that would place an order. So, to offset irrelevant searches, you can add the word *game* as a negative keyword.

In order to make a word be a negative word in Google search, you need to add a minus sign before each word you want to not trigger a search. (So, if we want to target the negative word *game* to follow this rule, we define the keyword to be *-game*.)* *

Text Ads

Did you know that the average person who does a search spends about 3 seconds before they click on a result? We briefly mentioned earlier how search ads are text based (while search shopping ads can have some images included). Since all you have to convince someone to click on your ad is the text, you need to take advantage of that fact by making your text ad compelling. The best practices for doing that are:

1. Have a **call to action**: A call to action is any active verb you can insert into your ads that will compel people to take action. Common active verb call to actions are: discover, learn more, buy, shop, book, join, register, signup, call, message, plan etc.
2. Include the keyword you're targeting in the ad: When the word the user searches for appears in the ad text, it appears bolded which makes it more prominent to click on. This can also improve your quality score (more on what that is later). The way this is done, is if you're targeting the keyword *cheese pizza*, have the keyword *cheese pizza* mentioned in your ad at least once.
3. Mention your selling points: Since users spent such a small amount of time on the search engine before they click, you need to highlight what makes you unique in your text ad, that includes prices, promotions and any other competitive advantage you can highlight on why someone should choose you.
4. Intercapitilization: I found that making the first letter of each word in an ad capital, can increase its click through rate (CTR, i.e. how many people click on the ad as a percentage) go up by up to 20%! That's because words appear more prominently when you write them in all caps. So instead of writing "Get the best pizza in town", you should write it as "Get The Best Pizza In Town". This technique is known as intercapitilization or camel case, and although it is not grammatically correct, it can have a positive effect, especially for search ads.
5. Exclamation point: I recommend to also include one exclamation mark in your ad (preferably at the end), since that gives it another attention-grabbing dimension.

Ad Automation

If you're running a large number of ads one popular technique to streamline the ad creation process is to use automation. For search ads, this can be done through:

Dynamic search ad, which are ads created automatically by linking to parts of your website. For example, if you have a new collection of items you want to market that may change every once in a while, you can have the text of the ad change depending on your featured product (so the ad text will mention the exact model of product being promoted). **Dynamic Keyword Insertion,** this is a process by which you can create ads that change depending on the keyword that was searched for. For example, if you're selling dozens of sizes for a pair of shoes, you can have the ad automatically change depending on what size was searched for, without having to create dozens of ads. So, if a user searches for size 12 it will show them an ad for size 12, if they search for a size 8, it will show them size 8 and so on.

Quality Score

One of the most important things you need to know about search ads, is that even though you are bidding in an auction, there are rules. Mainly one rule, called the **quality score.** When you bid on any keyword a quality score (from 1 to 10) is given to that keyword based on how relevant the search engine thinks you are to that keyword.

Why is this done?

The main reason is because search engines want to stay relevant and provide useful searches for people. Imagine if you searched for "flights to paris" and were greeted with ads on "investing in the stock market." What would you do? Most likely you would search to another search engine, or if you're not aware that you were served an ad, you'd probably have the impression that the search engine you used wasn't providing good results. That's why for a search engine the integrity of their search results is always their number 1 priority, and that's why the quality score matters.

Bidding

Let's take a look at what the bidding auction looks like when we're running search ads (which have to take into account the bid and the quality score), which looks like this:

Ad Rank = Bid X Quality Score

Advertiser A	Bids $1 CPC	Has a Quality Score of 1	Loses the auction
Advertiser B	Bids $0.5 CPC	Has a Quality Score of 10	Wins the auction

Quality Score

Unlike with Display ads, since Search ads also depend on your Quality Score, it is very common for someone to pay less, but still be on top in the ad search results, if they have a higher Quality Score.

As a result of this, by having a high Quality Score, you actually end up paying less!

Advertiser A	Bids $1 CPC	Has a Quality Score of 1	Loses the auction
Advertiser B	Bids $0.5 CPC	Has a Quality Score of 10	Wins the auction

Quality Score Bidding

Again, the same rules apply as mentioned in the display section (you only have to pay just enough to beat the person underneath you in the auction). However, this time, it's possible to pay more than the person who has a higher search result than you do, just because they have a higher quality score.

Improving your Quality Score

So now, you're probably sold on the benefits of increasing your Quality Score, so how can you do that? Keep in mind, that the purpose of the Quality Score, is to make sure your ad is relevant and useful for people searching for your keywords. Therefore, to increase quality score, you mainly need to focus on:

1. **Ad Relevancy** Having your ad be relevant to your keyword (for example, mentioning the keywords you're targeting in the ad)
2. **Keyword Specificity** Make your keywords more specific by using narrower match types. For example, bidding on *white laptops* as an exact match keyword will have a better quality score than bidding on *laptops* as a broad match keyword (if you're selling white laptops).
3. **Landing Page Relevancy** Having your website (landing page, the first page the user goes on after clicking the ad), be relevant to the ad (for example, if the ad is about white laptops, make the landing page have white laptops on it),
4. **Landing Page Performance** Make sure your website loads quickly and is optimized for all devices (especially mobile devices)
5. **Ad Quality**: Make your ads more compelling. That means writing better ad copy to make people want to click on your ad, since the more people that click on your ad, the higher your Quality Score will be.

Digital - Long Term Marketing

This is where you use free techniques to grow the number of visitors and customers you get in an organic way. Content Marketing and Inbound Marketing (terms which we'll talk about in more detail later) both fall underneath this. The idea behind this approach is that you want to set up systems in place that allows you to organically (without paying) scale up your efforts. However, instead of paying with money to essentially buy traffic (like is the case with Push and Pull marketing), you need to work on content (videos, blog articles, social media etc.) which takes a lot of time and patience. The two main channels that fall under this category are organic search engine traffic (SEO) and organic social media.

Organic Traffic

People finding their way to you, which could be from **SEO (Search Engine Optimization)** which is getting your website to organically (without paying) rank high on the search engine, getting traffic from partner websites / organizations, or by spreading through **branding** or **word of mouth** to an extent where you are getting people coming to you on their own.

SEO

Search engines (Google, Bing, Baidu, and Yandex) are the largest sources of organic (free) traffic online. SEO (Search Engine Optimization), is the process by which you can optimize your website to get more traffic and rank higher on search engines. This mainly involves 4 steps.

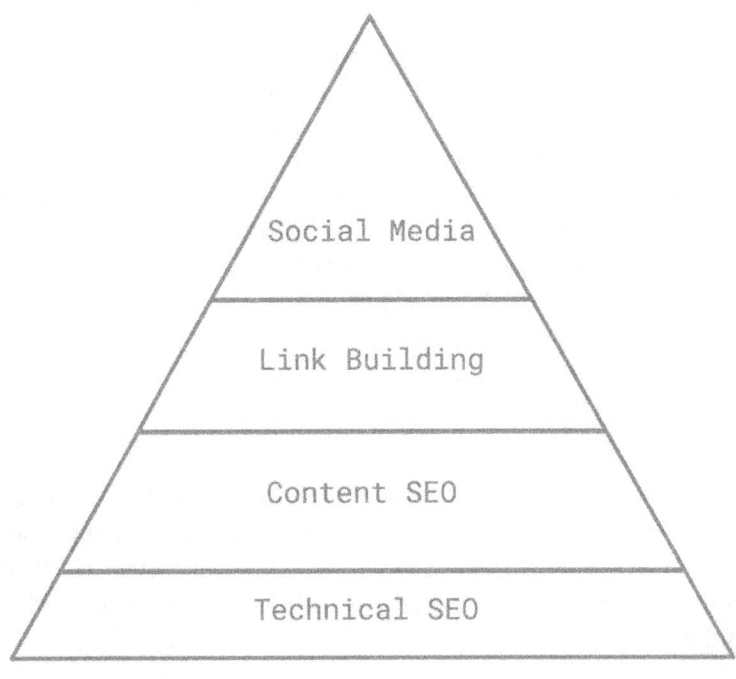

SEO Pyramid

We'll be going over more of the technical details in Chapter 6 and show you how to actually make changes to impact each of these sections. For now, though, here are the main sections that encompass organic traffic from search engines.

Technical SEO: This has to do with making sure that your website is properly found by the search engines. It involves making sure all of your pages can be found by implementing setting on your website, and also making sure you don't have any penalties that would prevent your site from showing up or ranking high (for example, slow load times, or duplicate content). Usually technical SEO is done by your development or technical team.

Content SEO: This involves creating optimizing the content (words on your pages), to ensure that the words you want to rank for are ones your website includes. For example, if you're selling *cheese* *pizza*, you need to make sure that that you put the word *cheese pizza* in all of the right places on your website to make sure the search engine knows to rank you for that keyword.

Link Building: One of the trends that made search engines popular from the late 90's onwards, was the idea that if one website has a link to another website, it's like a vote of credibility. This idea was first popularized by Google and their *Page Rank* algorithm. The idea behind this is that the more people that link to a page, the higher value that page is, and therefore the higher its ranking should be. Link building is the process of finding and optimizing those opportunities by trying to create as many links as possible point towards your website so that it ranks higher in Google searches.

Social Media in SEO: The last area to focus on for SEO is Social media. Social media doesn't have as strong an impact as the other 3 areas discussed so far, but it still has a minor spill over effect that if capitalized on, can yield very positive results for your search engine ranking.

Organic Social Media

This is where you build a community of followers to join your tribe, which could be people following your social accounts, joining a group you own (Facebook group, Slack group, Discord channel, Meetup group etc.), or on a personal level becoming an **influencer** that drives traffic to your business

Digital - Retention Marketing

The final category of digital marketing is retention marketing. This basically involves retaining (keeping) customers and users that already interacted with you (by buying from you or visiting your website), by showing them ads and re-engaging with them.

From what I've seen (working on various businesses and studies I've read), it is at least 5 times less expensive to keep an existing customer than to find a new customer. That is why retention marketing is so crucial. If you want to build a sustainable digital marketing strategy, you have to focus on retention! The channels that fall underneath retention marketing are:

Email Marketing

Think about how many social media networks have come and gone in your life, in just the last 10 years. Myspace, Friendster, even Facebook now is on the decline for many. However, there is one communication channel that has so far proved to be so "antifragile" that it has existed in the consumer space since the early 90's and has no sign of decline. If anything, it has actually significantly increased in popularity in recent years. That channel of course is email. With email marketing, you own your audience. You don't have to rely on any third part community. An example that severely affected a lot of marketers was when Facebook changed their algorithm on how Facebook business pages show data to users. Now, page likes on Facebook are almost meaningless in terms of the amount of organic traffic they generate. Reach on Facebook (how many people see your posts when you post something on a company page), now is on average between 1-4%! That means that if you run a Facebook page with 1,000 fans and you post something on your page, on average your post will only be seen by 10 to 40 people! If you contrast that to email, when you send out an email blast to your list of 1,000 emails, if you have a healthy list, you'll get an open rate of 20-30% on average, which is between 200-300 people! So, you can see how controlling your email list has been and continues to be the most robust and scalable way to build your online community.

Within email marketing, there are 2 main ways in which you can engage with your audience. The first way is through traditional **newsletters** otherwise known as email blasts, e-shots or e-newsletter. This is what people typically think about whenever they think about email marketing. It's pretty straight forward. It basically entails having a list of emails and sending them emails. The other more complex way is through **automated emails**. These are also known as **Drip** campaigns, or **Transactional** emails. These differ from normal email newsletters, by instead of having a list that you just send to, instead you have emails that are only sent whenever certain conditions are met. For example, you can send out an email automatically whenever anyone subscribes to you online, or contacts you. Then you could schedule a second email, which would go to the same person one week (or based on any other condition you define) after they open the first email. The series of steps you define is known as a **workflow**. We'll talk about how these work in greater detail later in this book.

Messaging Platforms

Even though email is the most famous and robust way to grow an audience for retention marketing, there are other various ways in which you can build out a list. One way this is done is through other apps, or via phone numbers. If you have a database of user phone numbers, you could send them SMS's directly. You could also use messaging apps that allow you to send users mass messaging for free, like WhatsApp, WeChat, or Telegram. You could also have a list that is directly tied to a messaging app, like Facebook messenger. Now Facebook messenger is a really effective app to build an audience through, however its main drawback is the fact that it does not give you direct access to the emails / phone numbers of the community you collect. Therefore, it ties you down to only use their platform, which could at any moment change (it's not an audience that you fully own). However, it can still be a good option when used wisely. A great feature that Facebook messenger has is **Chatbots**. This feature allows you to create automated messages that react to what users type in. For example, you could send out a broadcast message with a few if you products to your list on Facebook messenger (using software like ManyChat or ChatFuel), and then once a user opens the message in the Messenger app, allow them to choose the product they want to learn more about.

This is similar to the workflow example I gave earlier for Drip campaigns, since it allows you to create decision trees where you allow users to choose to learn more with what interests them and interact with you in an automated way. It still hasn't reached the stage for the mass market where you can decipher what a user types in; having a decision tree in the form of a chatbot workflow, however, is a great way to automate and customize the messages you send out.

Remarketing

Remarketing (also known as Retargeting, and yes there is virtually no difference between those two words), is a form of digital marketing that allows you to target people that already interacted with you in the past. These could be people that visited your website but didn't complete a purchase, or it could be people that visited one of our social media channels. You may know this as those annoying ads that follow you across the internet, because you looked at product once. Although they may be annoying, they can be incredibly effective if done right. The way it works is that every time a user visits your website (or social media channel), you can store them in something known as an audience list. This audience list is cookie-based, meaning that it stores the user data based on a tiny file that it drops on the user's browser. What this means is that the user doesn't even need to log in to have the ad follow them. Out of all of the paid channels listed here, this channel is the most effective (in terms of how cost effective it is), but it has limitations built into it. If you have an eCommerce store (or business that has dozens, hundreds or thousands of products), you can also create **Dynamic remarketing** ads. These are ads that can be created automatically based on a **product feed**. For example, if you're selling laptops and you have hundreds of models, you could use dynamic remarketing ads to automatically create hundreds of variations of your ads, so that if someone browses on one or multiple laptop products, you'll follow them with a custom ad when they leave your site, that has the exact products they browsed on!

Audience Targeting

Another way to retain your customers is to target them with ads, but through audiences that you upload. The way this works is that you gather a list of customer data, like emails or phone numbers. You can then take that data and upload it to any of the "Push" marketing channels we discussed earlier (Google Display Network, Facebook Ads etc.). What happens then, is that your ad will only be shown to users whose data you already have. This is an effective way to market, because you are showing your ads to an already warm audience, and not trying to market to someone that may or may not be interested in what you're offering. If you define an audience, you can now also create on many paid platforms something called a **Lookalike audience**, which is a larger audience created using machine learning, by looking for patterns in your existing audience. For example, if you upload a list of 1,000 customers onto an ad platform (like Google or Facebook), it can create an audience 50 times the size of that audience by using machine learning and looking for patterns you might not have noticed in the audience. By using its own algorithms, it can create a larger list and expand who it recommends that you target. This larger list will share attributes that your customers have.

It might give you a new audience that is now 50,000 people, by finding commonality in random areas (maybe you sell flowers and your customers all like to play golf or croquet for example. Things you may never have thought about!).

Channel Conclusion

We covered a lot of channels in this section, and when into quite a bit of detail with some of them (mainly Push and Pull marketing). For others (like Long term marketing channels and retention channels), we'll be going over them in a more granular practical way in upcoming chapters. For now, though, you should have a strong understanding about the fundamentals of the various digital marketing channels.

Chapter 3: Setting your foundations

The first step to getting started with Digital Marketing, is you have to lay the groundwork. Things have to be setup in such a way that you make sure you are tracking your spend and you know exactly how effective your efforts are. After all, that's one of the benefits of digital marketing, everything can be tracked! To do this, there are two main things you need to set up:

1. **Tracking Traffic** The sources of the traffic coming to your site / app is tracked.
2. **Tracking Conversions** Once people arrive onto your website / app, you are tracking value actions by them (otherwise known as goals or conversions)

Let's go over them in more detail.

Tracking Traffic

When a user visits your site or app, you want to know exactly where that user came from. There are many channels (as discussed earlier) and you need to know which of those channels brought you the traffic you're getting. The main way this can be segmented is **paid** versus **organic** traffic. With **paid** traffic, being from **Push** and **Pull** marketing channels (Google Ads, Facebook Ads etc.), and **organic** traffic being from **long term** and **retention** channels like organic social media, SEO, and email. It's important to know where traffic is coming from, from an overall, channel and individual campaign point of view. That way you can optimize by either trying new strategies or doubling down on what's working.

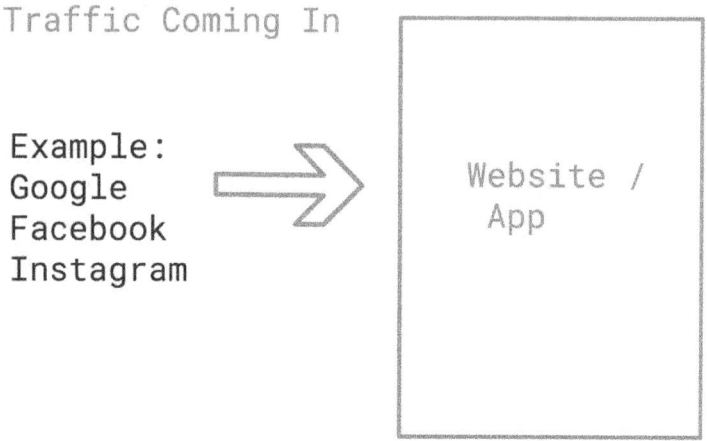

Incoming Traffic

The most famous free tool that people use for this is **Google Analytics**. Google Analytics is a tracking platform that can be installed for free on any application (as long as it's below 10 million hits per month, then it turns into a paid service). It allows traffic tracking on website and mobile apps. For digital marketers, it helps by showing you where your traffic is coming from by defining the **source** and **medium** of all of your traffic, with source being the website that referred the traffic, and medium being the means by which it reached you from that source. For example, if a piece of traffic comes from Google Ads, it will mark the source as Google, and medium as CPC (which is the way you pay for the ad, more about this later). However, if a piece of traffic came from normal Google Search (i.e. not an ad), it will show up as source Google and medium Organic.

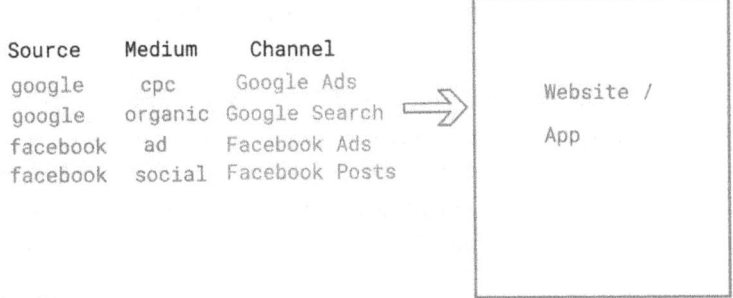

Source Medium

Tracking Non-Google Traffic

However, this only works if you are tracking a Google channel. If you want to track a non-Google channel using Google Analytics, you have to first tag the URL, which entails adding some information to the URL, which allows the source and medium to be tracked.

Example of a tagged URL

https://astrolabs.com/?utm_source=facebook&utm_medium=ad&utm_-campaign=summer-campaign

Why do you need to do this? It has to do with how traffic is tracked online. On the internet, when traffic from one site goes to another site, the site that it goes to knows what the source site is, but not much else. Since the rest of the internet is not tracked by your site, it doesn't know how it came from other sides. The exception to this is Google, since Google knows what happens on its platform, so it can tell you the Medium information.

Tracking Conversions

The next important thing you need to track, are your conversions. What is a conversion? A conversion is any action on your site / app, that you define as valuable for your business. People also refer to this as a goal, an action, a transaction or even a sale. Usually, this means monetarily valuable.

For example, if I'm running an eCommerce business, for me a conversion would be someone makes a purchase on my site. If I'm running a freelance consultancy service, a conversion would be having a client signup through my site. It could also be something that doesn't directly pay me money but is eventually valuable for my business. An example of this is if I get a customer lead (their email, or phone number) on my site, that would be valuable to me, since I would know that some of those leads would turn into paying customers. A conversion could also be something that doesn't directly bring in money but may lead to growth for your business. Content is an example of this.

If you have a news website, or some blog or content site, your goal may just be to increase viewership or readership, since that brings in more eyeballs, which allows you to eventually change subscriptions or run more ads. In cases like that, a conversion may be how long a person stays on your site or app, or how many pages or sections the go on. A modern-day example of this is Netflix. For Netflix, not only is a conversion getting someone to sign up for Netflix, but they also want to make their platform be "sticky" i.e. a place where people stay for a long time, since for Netflix's case, although they don't directly run ads on the platform, the more engaged people are with their service, the more loyal a customer base they'll have, and the more attractive they'll be to court other shows and content creators for exclusive rights.

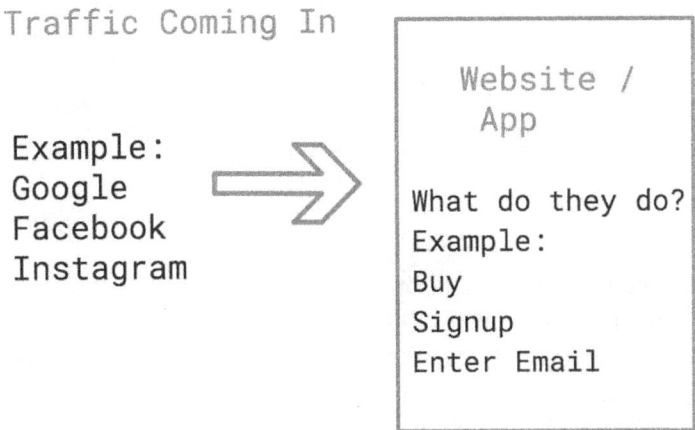

Traffic Conversion

Of course, the type of conversion you'll want to track depends on your business model and your business objectives, but just keep in mind that you will need to have some end goal to what you're doing.

There are two main types of conversions or goals you would want to track: There are 2 kinds of results that are measured in Digital Marketing:

Performance Goals

Performance goals are results that are measured based on how many desirable results happen for your business. What is a desirable result? Usually this takes the form of something that leads to a positive effect on your bottom line, mainly either leads or sales. These results are usually known as goals, transactions or conversions.

From my experience, the three main types of performance goals are either:

a. **Purchases:** These are the most common types of performance goals, in which you have a product or a service that you directly sell online. This can be anything that falls under the eCommerce category or is something that can be purchased online.
   b. **Signups:** If you have a service people need to sign up for, like a subscription service or an offline event, that can also be a form of a performance goal.
   c. **Leads:** Either Email or Phone numbers gathered. This can be from your site or directly through social media (through lead forms). If you're selling to businesses (B2B - Business to Business), then you may also have another step in this process where you link the leads generated to your own CRM (Customer Relationship Management) software, which you can then follow up through your sales team.

Awareness Goals

Goals that have to do with raising awareness for a product / service but are not as concerned with directly measure the impact of marketing spend ROI (return on investment). Examples of awareness goals are:

- **Impressions**

(Views on your posts / ads) This is where you focus on people seeing your ad (getting your ad in front of as many eyeballs as possible).

- **Video views**

This is similar to impressions, but instead of people just viewing the ad, you also track their watch time. You may have seen these types of ads on YouTube that you skip (known as TrueView ads) or that you are forced to watch (bumper ads), or on any social media channel like Facebook or Instagram. These video ads can either be charged on an impression basis or on a video view basis. The difference is that impressions are charged if the video loads, but video views are charged only if a certain criterion is met (they watch a certain amount of the video).

- Engagement (comments, likes etc.)
Another type of goal you might track are engagement goals. This is where you optimize for how often your ads or posts get commented on or interacted with (for example comments on social media posts).

- Followers
The final way in which you can be charged is to pay to get more followers. Getting followers is the definition of a vanity metric (something that looks good but doesn't on its own provide any real value). This could be through "shady" means, like searching "buy followers" online and paying a company to get you likes (which of course I do not recommend, since those followers will bring 0 engagement) or by buying followers through platforms themselves (through Facebook, Twitter, LinkedIn etc. directly). In the world of performance marketing (where you're selling a product or service) I think that buying followers is a waste of money, especially because engagement on most social media platforms is very low.

For Facebook for example, if you post something on your page, on average only about 1-2% of your audience will even see it! This may be a little higher on other channels like LinkedIn, Twitter, and Instagram, but it's still a challenge, so keep in mind that if you have 1,000 followers, it doesn't mean 1,000 people will see everything you post. Usually only a fraction will. There is another reason why I am against buying followers from third party sources, is that when you buy followers, it permanently changes the makeup of your audience. Since your audience builds off of itself (by automatically suggesting your page to those that are likely to follow it), this has a negative impact on your organic growth if the followers are not actually people interested in your product. It also negatively impacts paid campaigns you might run in the future if you want to try things like Lookalike Audiences (targeting people that the algorithm thinks are similar to your existing followers). In general,

I don't recommend it.

Having said that though, there are still a couple of reasons why I would actually recommend that you buy followers.

1) If you want to become an influencer. I know this is a fad at the moment, but you would be surprised at how many influencers at least buy a seed audience (the first thousand followers or so), in order to get into the game, as it's a lot easier to organically go from 1,000 to 2,000 followers, then to go from 0 to 1,000 followers (it's easier to get followers if you're already popular).

2) If your business is heavily focused on social media and content (news sites, blogs etc.) I might consider (at least initially) buying followers in that case, since you want to have an audience that regularly shares and engages with your content.

In either case though, my natural reaction is to be against buying social media followers, however if you feel there is a strong need for it, I would be cautious and only do it through the platforms directly and not use a third party service, since if you do it through the platforms directly they let you choose the types of followers you would want to gain, based on their interests and demographic data, which would lead to you having a follower base that is more likely to engage and interact with your content.

Awareness Goals Conclusion

Awareness goals are usually prioritized in businesses where no action can be taken online. In such cases, the purpose of the marketing efforts is branding, so a purchase can be made offline. For example, if Pepsi wants to advertise their products online, their end goal is not for someone to buy a soft drink online, but rather to have the brand be ingrained in their head, so the next time they're given a choice, they choose Pepsi in the grocery store.

I usually only recommend to focus on awareness goals under a few circumstances, mainly if either you are

a. A large company that doesn't directly sell anything online (like Mercedes or Coca Cola)
b. A company or organization with a large budget that wants to hype a product launch
c. You want to raise awareness and then drive them down the funnel (using Audience lists)
d. You want to target a small demographic or group, by running ads via customer lists (for example, targeting people after they watch one of your social media videos through **engagement audiences**)
e. You're a content website or social media company or influencer

Focusing On Performance Goals

For most businesses, instead of awareness goals, I would highly recommend to focus on is performance goals. Since they are goals in which you can track the ROI (return on investment), which is the cost and revenue associated with that marketing campaign. These are goals that you can directly measure online. As mentioned earlier, examples of performance goals are:

- Online Sales
- Online bookings
- Online signups
- Leads generated (usually emails or phone numbers)
- Subscriptions
- Any new customers

You can see from these examples, that performance goals are more tangible. That's why if you're selling any product or service, whether that's B2B (business to business) or B2C (business to consumer), it's usually always better and most cost effective to focus on performance goals. Focusing on performance goals is usually called **performance marketing**.

Tracking Performance Goals

There are two main types of performance goals in the digital marketing world that you can track **Destination URLs** and **Events**.

Destination URLS

The easiest and most popular way to track a performance goal is by using a destination URL as your goal. The way this works is by having a page that a user would also be able to visit if they completed the performance goal, and just count the number of visits on that page.

For example, if a user completes a purchase on an eCommerce site, they are usually taken to a **thank you page** (a page which confirms their order). In order to track a performance goal in that case, all you have to do is track the number of times that thank you page gets visited.

Conversion Funnel

You may have several steps a user has to take before they can reach the final thank you page. If you want to count all of the steps, along with the drop off rate of each step, you can do so by tracking your **conversion funnel** (also known as a **goal funnel**). The simplest funnel is just one with two steps. They visit your website and they convert.

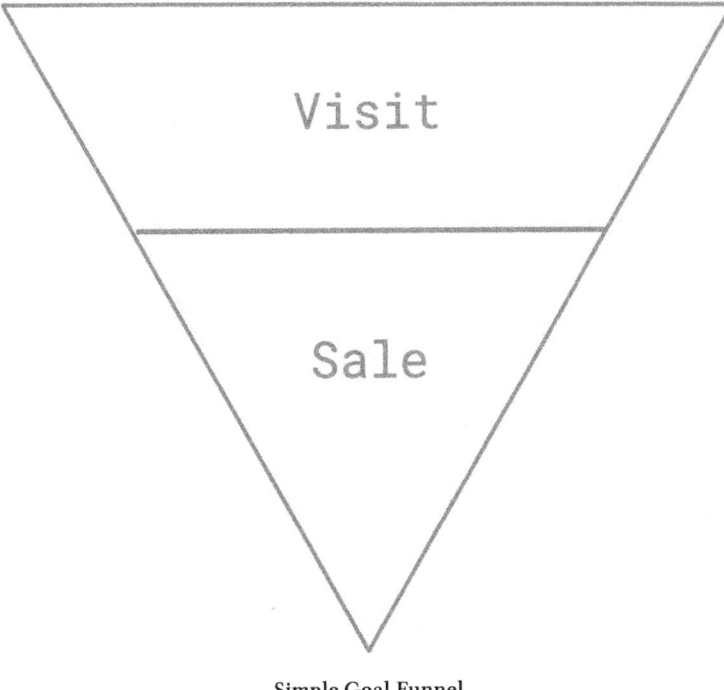

Simple Goal Funnel

The difference in percentage between these two steps is your **conversion rate**. For example, if you get 100 visits, and 2 sales, then your conversion rate is 2%.

For eCommerce, the most common example of this is when you have an online shopping cart. In that case, your conversion funnel will typically have 3 steps (4 if you count the page before they add to their cart):

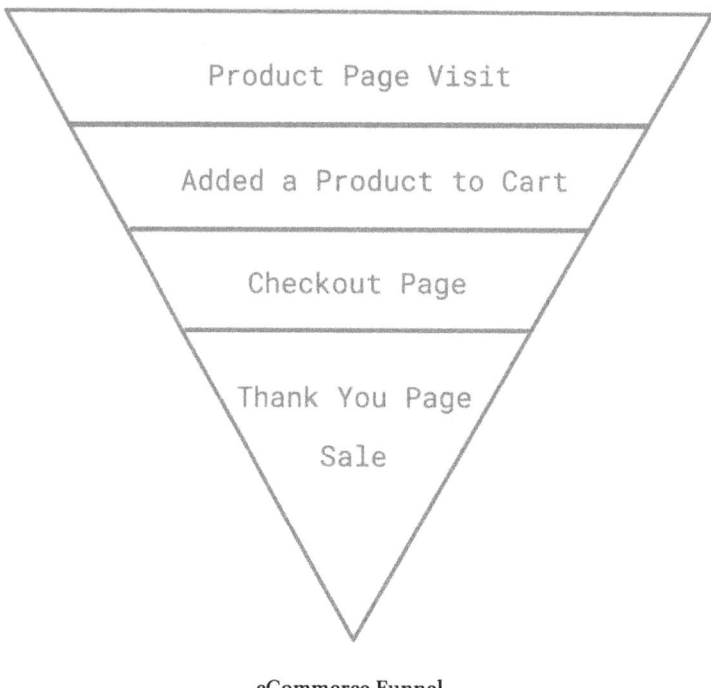

eCommerce Funnel

1. Cart Page
2. Checkout Page
3. Thank You Page

Events

The other popular way to calculate a performance goal is by tracking an **event**. An event is any action that you want to track on a website or app that does **not** make the URL change. For example, let's say your website has a contact form on it. If a user submits the contact form one of two things could happen. Either the URL changes to a thank you page, in which case I can calculate the number of conversions by just counting how many times that page was visited (as outlined in the previous example), or the URL does not change. If the URL does not change (or if it's an app and it does not load another screen), then I have to track that action as an event. Events are not tracked by default in most tracking solutions (like Google Analytics), so they need additional setup.

You may be wondering, why you have to do this in the first place. Shouldn't this be automatically tracked? Well, the reason why you need to do this is because by default most tracking solutions only track **page views** which mean that they also detect if a URL or screen changes in your website or app. Because of that, any action that happens on page (like a form submit, watching a video, etc.) needs to be tracked through events.

Custom Code

The first way to implement an event is by adding a piece of custom code to the event you want to track. This is something that is usually done by your web developer or your technical team. The way it works is that an **event tracking** code will be added to whatever item you want to track, which sends that event to your tracking software. For example, if you want to track if a form is filled out, without the URL changing, then you add an event tracking code to the form submit button in the HTML code (this is done through JavaScript, through something known as the data layer).

Auto-Event Tracking

The easier way to track event it to have them tracked automatically without having to add any custom code. However, as I mentioned most tracking platforms cannot out of the box automatically track events. However, there are a couple of options to make it easier for you to track event automatically.

1. The first way is to use a paid event tracking solution. There are several options I list in the tools section referenced at the

end of this book.

2. The second way (which is free) is to implement **Auto-Event Tracking** using a Tag Manager. The way this works is that an event tag is added that automatically tracks all events based on an action you define. That could be a click, a scroll, or a form submission for example. Then, you can automatically send all event actions relevant to you into your tracking solution. For example, if you have a form on the homepage of your website you want to track, by implementing Auto-Event Tracking you can automatically know that the exact form you want to track was filled.

The most common way to do this is by using Google Tag Manager (I'll discuss this in more detail later in this chapter).

Ad Platform Pixels

Besides tracking your overall conversion goals (using a tool like Google Analytics), you may also want to add the tracking codes of the individual ad platforms to your website as well. For example, if you're running Facebook ads, you would add the Facebook ads tracking code to your website (another name for this is a pixel).

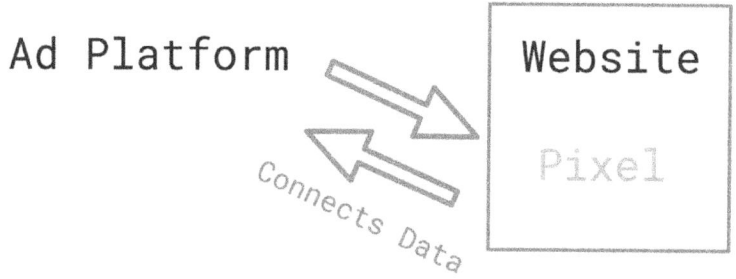

Ad Platform Pixel

What is the point of this? Mainly it serves the following purposes:

1. It creates a bridge between your site and the ad platform (which allows you to share data between the ad platform and your website)

2. It allows you to create remarketing lists and connect them directly to your ads

3. It allows you to turn on conversion tracking on the ad platform (which allows you to view directly on the ad platform which ad brought a conversion, instead of always having to check Google Analytics) and also turn on CPA bidding. For example, if you connect the Facebook pixel to your website, it will allow you to bid on a CPA (cost per acquisition basis), so your bids and targeting will be optimized for conversions.

Tag Managers

If you start running a lot of ads across many marketing channels, you'll come across a common problem. There are a lot of tags or pixels (i.e. pieces of codes) that you have to keep adding to your website. If you want to track conversions on Facebook Ads, you have to install the Facebook pixel, if you want to track conversion on Google Ads, you have to install the Google pixel, if you want to track conversions on LinkedIn, you have to install the LinkedIn pixel etc.

It's not just limited to conversion tracking on ad platforms either. One example I gave earlier in this chapter, was how if you want to track events on your website, it's also required that you to install a piece of code. Another example is if you want to install other marketing tools, such as a subscriber popup for your newsletter or a share button for social media. All of those examples need you to install a piece of code (or pixel) on your website.

Without A Tag Manager

```
Website

Facebook Pixel
Google Ads Pixel
LinkedIn Pixel
Twitter Pixel
Google Analytics
```

Without A Tag Manager

The problem with keep having to add these pixels is:

1. It requires you to constantly having to update your code. If you're not a developer this could be time consuming and potentially costly (in terms of development costs and time).

2. It makes your page load slower. If you load all of the pixels on your own site, it can slow down your site load time.

3. It doesn't give you flexibility of the data layer. So for example, if you want to implement event tracking, you would

Using a Tag Manager solves all of these issues, since it allows even non-developers to easily add marketing pixels to websites, it has options to load pixels (tags) in a smart way so the page loads faster, and it also allows you to send data across tags (such as the case for

Auto-event tracking).

With A Tag Manager

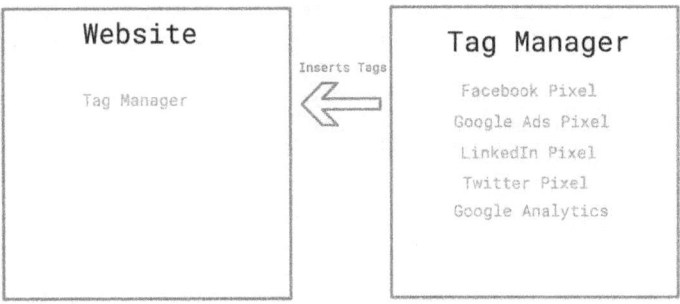

With A Tag Manager

Tracking B2B versus B2C

Another common concern people have when it comes to tracking digital marketing performance goals has to do not with the goals themselves but rather with the nature of their businesses. I often hear people say, that may work for B2C (business to consumer, where you're selling a product / service to the general public), but my business is B2B (business to business, where you sell your product / service to other businesses), so it these techniques don't apply. I have to disagree.

You see, when it comes to B2B it has the same tactics as B2C and the same overall philosophy. The only difference is that instead of selling something directly, you first gather lead, and then usually follow up with them with your sales team through a combination of emails, phone calls and meetings, all of which is usually tracked in some kind of a CRM system (a customer management system used to keep track of your sales prospects).

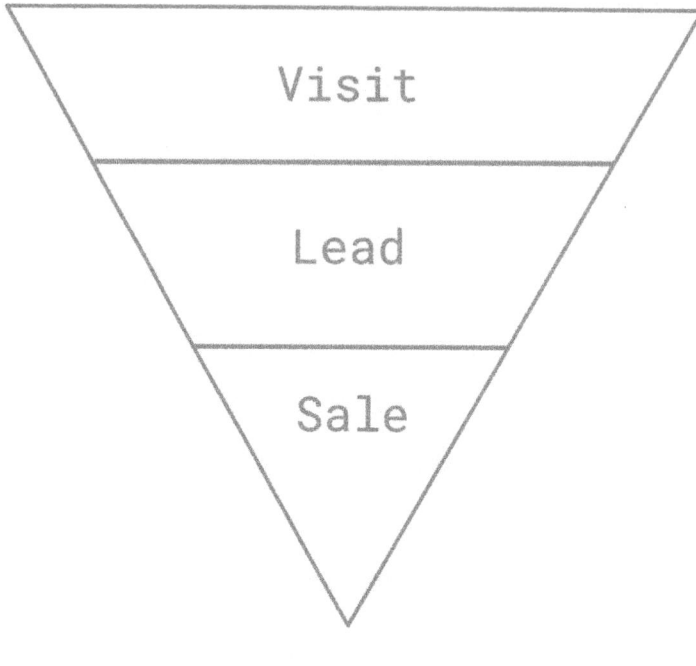

B2B Funnel

So, in reality the only thing that changes is your funnel, you just add another step, which is your sales process, or the process by which you convert a lead into a sale. In terms of marketing, the same channels, tracking and strategies still work, however usually B2B businesses put more of a focus on in-person traditional sales.

Action Plan

Disclaimer: Some of the items listed here require you to follow step by step technical guides. Including them in this book would have made this book very long, and also outdated very quickly (since the steps often change). However, I'd still like to help you implement the recommendations in this book, so I'll share the latest guides and resources for all of the items listed here on a website that I'll keep updated (http://tools.timelessdigitalmarketing.com). If I mention "see tools", it means to check that link.

1. Signup for a tracking platform (I recommend Google Analytics) and install it on your website.
2. Choose at least 2 performance goals that are important for your business (sales, leads, newsletter signups etc.)
3. Track those performance goals either through destination URL's or events (see tools).
4. Setup eCommerce tracking if you have an eCommerce website (see tools)
5. Track the performance of your goals from Google Analytics
6. Install a tag manager (like Google Tag Manager)
7. Install the pixels for any ad platforms you are using (Facebook, Google etc.)

Chapter 4 - How to NOT waste money!

Ok, you must be thinking "So I want to do digital marketing, but how do I not waste money?" Maybe you even tried some Facebook ads before and they didn't work. I understand the skepticism, and I definitely believe that you can waste a ton of money on digital marketing if you don't do things correctly, but that's what this book is for. To help you avoid the common pitfalls and help you not waste any money. Luckily, digital marketing works in such a way where you don't have to spend money and hope things will work out. You can be very systematic about your strategy, and only scale once things start to work.

Budgets

The trick is that you have to work in a way where you are making back what you're spending. It's as simple as that. This is done by starting at the end. Since your marketing budget is a variable cost you have to figure out what spend makes sense. This is one of the most common questions people ask. What is a good budget? How much should I start with? How do I know if I'm spending too much or too little? The answer I always give is that your revenue from marketing should be much higher than the amount it costs to gain that revenue.

Revenue from marketing should be greater than Marketing Spend. This is the essence of **Performance Marketing** (marketing done where you track the performance of your efforts in direct correlation to their business impact, i.e. how to make back more than you spend!).

This seems fairly obvious, but what about your other expenses?

Salaries, fixed costs, licensing fees, shipping costs and more?

A more accurate formula to use would look like:

Revenue from marketing should be MUCH greater than Marketing Spend.

That way when you take your Revenue and subtract all of the other costs you're left with some Net Profit at the end.

Ok, so you might think that it makes sense in theory, but how do you actually go about defining how much to spend to test for my business?

There are a few things to keep in mind.

You may already have a budget

If you work for a larger company, you will probably have a set marketing budget. Where did this marketing budget come from? Most likely it was put there whenever the leadership team in your company was coming up with their projections. It most likely will be based on past performance, and a rough estimate of the optimal level to spend on marketing before you notice diminishing returns. Based on what I've seen, this marketing rate is typically between 5-20% of top line gross revenue. It could go up and it could go down, but that's typically the number I see.

You don't have a budget

What if you don't have a budget though? In that case. you have to come up with your own optimal spend, but this will be more in a testing environment. In this scenario, what's more important than budgets are your costs that are tied to percentage of revenue and profit, which is calculated by looking at something known as your **Cost Revenue Ratio** (which is Costs / Revenue as a percentage). Whenever you're first starting off with your digital marketing, you should have a number set as a maximum, where anything spent past that on marketing would be a negative on your business. For example, let's say that I'm selling a T-shirt. If I sell a T-shirt for $50 (that's my revenue), I don't make $50 profit. There are a lot of other costs I have to worry about. If we continue with this example, let's say that the shipping cost is $5, the packaging cost is $2, I pay $3 in taxes and I pay $20 a month to host my website (for the sake of simplicity, let's say I sell 20 shirts a month, so it costs roughly $1 in hosting costs to sell one shirt). So in reality, when I sell one shirt, my actual profit is: $50-(5+2+3+1)= $39 But hold on, we're forgetting something. I forgot to factor in marketing. In a perfect world people would just hear about me and buy my products on their own, but unfortunately, we don't live in that world and that's why this book exists. So, what we have to do is figure out what is an optimal rate for me spend on marketing. Let's take two scenarios.

Scenario 1

I make back my investment right away. In this scenario I want to make back the amount of money I'm spending right away and still have enough left over for me to be profitable as a business. As a rough rule of thumb, from what I noticed this percentage number is usually between 5-20% as I mentioned. Let's take a conservative number and say 15% on average. This is by no means a magic number, and you may notice that your number is lower or higher (hopefully lower not higher!), but it's a good indicator if it falls somewhere in that range. In this case, as an example, if I spent $15 in marketing, I want to immediately make back that amount by having a revenue of about $100. In my T-shirt example, if I'm selling my T-shirt for $50, that means that I'm probably willing to spend around $7.5 in marketing to sell one shirt. This $7.5 amount (the amount needed to make one sale), is defined as my **Cost per Acquisition** (CPA), which means that this is the amount of money needed to acquire one order. Now if I look at my overall profit per shirt (with a CPA of $7.5) it would look like this: $50-(5+2+3+1+7.5) = $31.5 Not bad for one sale.

Scenario 2

The other option I have is to take a long-term approach of making my money back eventually, but not worrying about breaking even right away. This approach is riskier, but it can also be very profitable if done right. The idea in this scenario, is that you spend money upfront, with the hope of making back that money in the future, since you hope that you'll have enough brand loyalty and retention marketing to make people recurring customers. Let's go back to our T-shirt example and say that I have to spend $60 on marketing to get one sale of $50. On the surface this might seem like a horrible investment, and it very well may be. However, in certain cases it makes sense. For example, if you know that the average customer on your site (in their entire lifetime as a customer) purchases from you at least 3 times and their average order value per transaction is $50, then you spending $60 actually gets you a total revenue of $150, which makes a lot more sense. This concept of looking at the entirety of the revenue generated from a customer is known as the **Customer Lifetime Value** (also known as the CLV). This way of looking at your marketing throughout the entire lifetime of the customer means you want to track:

1. The amount it costs you to sign up a customer This is known as the **Customer Acquisition Cost** or **CAC**. Your objective is to make this number be as low as possible. It's calculated by looking at your total costs that you have to spend on

marketing to get one person to sign-up to become a customer or join your service. If you want to get even more granular, you can also look at this on a channel basis, so you'll see how much does it cost to get a customer per channel (for Facebook, Google etc.), and if you want to go even deeper you can look at what is your CAC on a marketing campaign level, or even on a demographic level (males versus females, or any other demographic profile you want to look at). The different groups or types of customers you look at are known as **cohorts**.

2. The total amount of revenue that you get from a customer
This is also known as the **Customer Lifetime Value** or **CLV**. The CLV value is calculated by looking at the average basket size (amount a customer pays) per transaction, and then multiplying that by the average number of sales that a customer makes on average in their lifetime (usually over years). For example, if the average price of the products I sell is $100 and from my data I know that the average customer buys 3 items (over a course of 2 years for example), then I'll know that my CLV is $300.

Another clear example that I'm sure you can relate to is that of Netflix or other similar subscription services that charge users on a monthly basis. Whenever you're doing marketing for this type of business, you don't only look at the amount of money gained by a user in a single month, but rather how much will a user make for you as long as they are a customer. So if Netflix charges $15 a month to users, and it has a CAC of $50 (how much it costs them to get turn someone into a customer through marketing), then it would take Netflix only 4 months ($15 x 4= $60) for them to turn a profit on average. So as long as the Customer Lifetime of their customers are more than 4 months, then they are profitable on the marketing costs. Of course then they have to break even on all of their other operational costs (licensing, server costs, salaries etc.), so they would need the CLV to be a lot higher than $60, which I assume based on what I hear it definitely is.

You might be thinking, ok this sounds interesting, but I'm just starting out, I have no idea what my CAC or CLV is, since I have no idea how many times my customers will buy from me! Fair enough. These calculations are usually done once your business has matured a bit and you already have some data. If you have no data, then you just have to make assumptions on how long you think a customer would be with you and how many times they would make a purchase. That's why it's always better to start tracking this data sooner rather than later. From what I've seen, if you have at least 6 months data, it's enough to get started seriously looking at the Customer Lifetime Value (in Chapter 10, I cover in detail how to calculate your CLV)

Ways to increase Customer Lifetime Value

Different businesses have different customers with different recurring buying behaviour for different goods and services. If you're selling something that someone only needs to buy once in their life, then you probably won't have high recurring revenue. However, there are ways that you can try to increase your customer lifetime value.

Turning your business into a recurring model business

This is the most lucrative, but also the hardest to pull off. Getting someone to agree to pay monthly is a lot harder of an ask than getting them to only buy once. However, this type of business works well particularly in the software, and content space (SAAS businesses and streaming sites for example), as well as with offline service businesses that work on retainers (like ad agencies). The main advantage in this business model is that is has the CLV built into it since you're charging on a monthly (or yearly) basis, it's really easy to calculate the CLV, you just need to look at what is the average time a customer stays with you, and multiply that by your recurring price. In world of recurring software businesses, this number is known as the **MRR** (monthly recurring revenue). What you need to be careful about for this model though, is the **churn** of your business (how many people are cancelling), since you always want your growth, to outstrip your lost recurring customers.

Build out your brand and unique selling points

Another way to get people to keep buying from you is to make them brand loyal. This ties into a customer's psychology and building trust. If you don't have a recurring model build into your business, then the only other way to get them to come back and tell their friends (to spread through word of mouth) is to have a superior product or service. You want to be so much better than competitors for whatever you offer that they automatically come back. This doesn't mean that you have to have complete dominance in a field. It could be just that you're the best in a very particular niche. For example, if you had a company that helped people get in shape through exercise videos, instead of trying to be the best exercise video provider in the world (which is hard to do because of how crowded it is), you could be the best in a very particular niche, like exercise videos for dads that have little time on their hands (which might be a great or horrible idea).

Net Promoter Score (NPS)

The idea is to have your product or service be so attractive that other people will share it with their friends and family. The way that this is calculated in companies is through something called the NPS, or net promoter score. The net promoter score is a value that you can calculate based on feedback from your customers (which is usually done through surveys). The way that is calculated is by asking a simple question (or a variant of the question): "How likely are you to recommend this product to a friend / co-worker?" You are then given a scale of 1 to 10. If your customers answer 9 or 10, they are promoters, if they answer 7 or 8, they are passives, and if they answer 1 to 6, then they are detractors. The easiest way that I found to calculate this, is to take the percentage of promoters and subtract from it the percentage of detractors (you ignore the passives). So for example, if you had 10 of your customers fill out your short survey, with 5 of them rating you a 10, 3 of them rating you a 7 and 2 of them rating you a 4, then your score would be: 50%-20%=30%

What is a good benchmark for this? It depends on a lot of factors like how externally facing is your brand, and how passionate you make your customers feel (which can change a lot depending on the industry, Google "NPS Benchmarks" to get tons of free data on this). From what I've seen, 70 is amazing (and only achieved by the most loved brands). The average for a normally liked brand is around 40, but again this varies significantly depending on the industry of the company.

Cross sell and expand your offering

Another area to be improved upon that can increase your customer lifetime value is to cross sell to your customer base and expand your offering. For example, if you sell someone a pair of sports shoes, they probably won't want to buy a pair of sports shoes for a while. However, they may be open to buy other types of shoes (for example dress shoes), or other items for their wardrobe. Also, maybe if you expanded what you offered, they may want that as well. For example, if they are into basketball and you started selling a new model of basketball shoes. Some items lend themselves to this more than others. Someone buying a book, will very likely want to buy other books, while other consumables limit recurring purchases. Some items encourage supplementary purchases as well. Just look at how Apple sells you on Airpods, wires and dongles after you buy their electronics. The point is that if you're smart about how your position your product and services, even if you have something that on its own is not needed more than once, you can always find other ways to get people to stay customers.

Planning Your Strategy

Now that you understand the main channels that you can go into in Digital Marketing, as well as how to think about budgeting when it comes to your business, how do you get started actually with actual marketing? There are two things you need to figure out so that you can get started creating a timeless digital marketing strategy.

1. You need to figure out how to get traffic quickly to your product / service to test and hone your offering, as well as to start getting in revenue for your bottom line. This is where we'll go over quick wins and strategies you can implement right away, to make sure that you see immediate benefits.
2. You need to build a sustainable system that works and grows your business in the long term. Some people refer to this as the "marketing flywheel" (a system that generates continuous growth long term).

These two approaches go hand and hand. The first one relies on using paid channels to get you optimized traffic (**outbound marketing**, or you going to people), and the second relies on organic means to generate traffic through partnerships and building out your own traffic (**inbound marketing**, or people coming to you).

The also boils down to 2 questions you need to ask yourself before you get started, which are:

1. What is the most I'm willing to spend to acquire one customer?
2. How fast do I want to grow

How much am I willing to spend to acquire a customer

The first question has to do with defining your: **CPA (Cost per acquisition)**: This is how much you're willing to spend to acquire one order as a marketing cost. If you work with leads that your sales team needs to follow up on, this would be known as your CPL (cost per lead).

OR, your...

CAC (Cost per acquisition of customer): This is how much you're willing to spend to acquire one customer as a marketing cost.

How fast do I want to grow?

In a perfect world, you would want to spend zero on marketing, but life isn't perfect. When it comes to digital marketing, there are two levers (or extremes) that you can go between). I've seen people that are very passionate about one or the other, with a gradient of anywhere in the middle. The two levers you can pull on are:

1. Short term gains (by paying money)
2. Long term gains (by paying with time)

What this means is that usually, if you want to get immediate results (sales by tomorrow or next week), you need to pay for it with money. If you want to get free traffic, then usually you have to invest a lot of time, and results are not seen for weeks, months and in some extreme cases even years.

You can be anywhere between these two extremes and where you are could change depending on your company priorities. At any moment in time you may feel more like one or the other or fluctuate between the two. For example, if there are situations where you are trying to meet your targets and you're on a deadline, you may temporarily spend more than usual on paid ads, in order to push a product or service, then after the promotion period is over, go back to your previous long term strategy. On the flip side, if you are currently using a paid advertising strategy, to get most of your customers, but you're spending too much on marketing, you might instead want to focus on longer term sustainable channels to bring down your marketing cost. There isn't a one size fits all solution, you have to iterate and choose what works best not just for your organization, but for your business's current needs. That's actually one of the best things about digital marketing, things are fluid and can be adjusted depending on your needs.

Action Plan

1. Define your profitable CPA number (see how I do this in scenario 1 and 2).
2. If you also care about leads for your business, also define your profitable CPL number
3. If your business is one where customers will buy multiple times, define what a profitable CAC number will be (see scenario 2).
4. Decide if you want short-term gains that you'll have to pay for, or if you'd like to focus on long term gains for lower costs

Chapter 5 - Getting Immediate Results

Let's start with the first level: Short term gains by paying money.

Creating Paid Campaigns

So, you decided that you want to create your first campaign. How do you choose a channel? How do you choose a budget? How do you start? So, before we define our **budget**, we need to run some tests. Basically, we need to figure out how our machine works and what is a reasonable Cost Per Acquisition for our efforts.

Testing Campaigns

Testing a campaign is kind of like a chicken and egg problem. You need data in order to know is a campaign is worth it for you, but you can only get that data if you already ran a campaign. If you're starting from scratch, to get over this issue I recommend you start by just running Push and Pull marketing ads (mainly on Google and Facebook) to spend at least $100 and run a campaign for at least 2 weeks. This could be higher or lower, but I found that running a 2 weeks campaign and spending at least $100, will usually give you enough data to make a decision on what a good budget is for you. Once you run a campaign you should know:

  i. Number of impressions (how many people saw your app)
  ii. Number of clicks / visits to your website / app
  iii. Number of conversions (signups, leads etc.)

iv. Amount spent (cost per ads)
v. Revenue (or estimated revenue) generated.

Once you have that you can figure out how much it would be expanded at a larger cost (by doubling or tripling the budget). Eventually though it will reach a plateau, since the size of your target audience is limited. Let's look now at how we'll define this audience.

Targeting- Starting with a Niche

Let's say that you're selling phone cases. Who would you start selling to? The first question you need to ask yourself, is who would be interested in this. In the beginning, it's actually better if this audience is as small as possible, the smaller the better! Why? Because you want to make sure that at least some people like it. If I take the phone case example, the first filter I'll put on it is, what is the minimum required to buy this product? First of all, they have to have some expendable income. Next they have to own the phone that I'm selling a case for (obviously), I can't sell them a case for an iPhone if they have a Samsung phone for example (unless let's say they're buying it as a gift).

Ok, now that you filtered out the minimum requirements, it's time to go deeper. You need to get so granular in your targeting that you actually envision that person. Give them a name, age, occupation, interests, likes and dislikes. In the marketing world, this is called a **customer persona**. Starting with a customer persona, helps you figure out exactly who your product or service is for, and allows you to be very specific in your targeting. This helps you in two ways:

1. It makes it easier for you to create marketing campaigns, both from defining your audience and targeting and writing the copy (text) of the ad.

2. It allows you to test your assumptions and see if your target persona actually is interested in what you offer.

If you try your best possible persona and you don't get any sales or leads and it's not profitable, that means that either you chose the wrong persona, or you need to make changes to your product (change the offering, price etc.)

So, what is needed in a persona? One way to think about it, is that you want to build a persona that is so detailed that you can actual picture that person in your head. It might be someone that you actually know in real life, or if you already have customers it may be modeled off of your most ideal customers.

Persona example

Let's give another example of a persona for a new eCommerce store. Since we're just starting out, we don't have any previous customers we can base this upon, so we have to come up with our persona. When thinking about a persona, there are a few fields that we need to define, and the more of these fields we have, the easier it will be for us to test. The ones that I recommend are:

· Name (a random name generated to make the person seem real)

· Gender (usually implied by the name)

· Age (an age range of +/- 5 years is fine too)

· Location (if you are active in multiple places, could be a country, city or neighborhood)

· Occupation (not always necessary, but can give more context into who you're targeting)

· Likes and dislikes (these can be directly related to the product, or can be more generic. We'll talk about how to tie these into your messaging)

· How they would use your product/ service (this is the typical use case, that is related to their likes / dislikes, which is either what the gain is that they want to get or what pain are they avoiding).

The following is an example of what a customer persona would look like:

Name: Sarah

Age: 28

Location: London

Occupation: Event Manager

Likes: Event Management, Concerts, Fashion Shows, Art

Dislikes: Common Fashion, Bad Quality, Expensive Retail

How would he/she use your product / service? She would use the product to wear for her casual outings or for normal workdays.

Ok so you may have noticed a few things about our customer persona:

1. We went very specific. We gave her a name (Sarah), an age, location and occupation. You may think this is going too far, but this actually helps us because it allows us to personalize our messaging in a way that is not possible when we think in generalities (otherwise we would be marketing to an abstract concept and not a real person in our mind).
2. Our likes and dislikes seem very different. This was done on purpose to show you two different approaches to think about likes and dislikes. You could go the route of tying it directly to the product, like we did for the likes, or you could make them be based on the behaviour of your target customer (which may not be tied directly to your product). Either approach you take helps you think personify your customers and allows you to target them in a much more effective way.

Now that we have a general idea of our profile, we can go about testing to see if this is an actual profile of our customer. For us to do this, we can target them either by using push marketing or pull marketing.

Push Marketing

The first way to reach our audience is through push marketing ads, mainly through ad networks and paid social media sites (like the Google Display Network, and paid social media sites like Facebook, as discussed in Chapter 2).

To start, let's discuss the overall way you should think about running your ads.

A funnel approach to your ads

When it comes to running your ads, you want to make sure that the campaigns you run work along the customer journey.

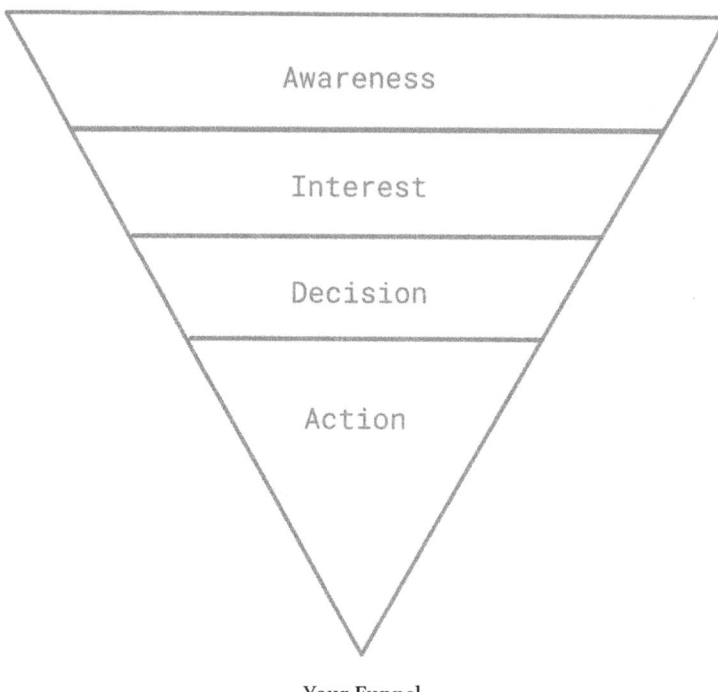

Your Funnel

The way this works practically is at the top of the funnel, you should ads that education users about your product or service, then you have ads that gauge their interest, and then finally you run ads that directly close the sale. All three of these steps can be done at once, but you can also run them as separate ad campaigns as well.

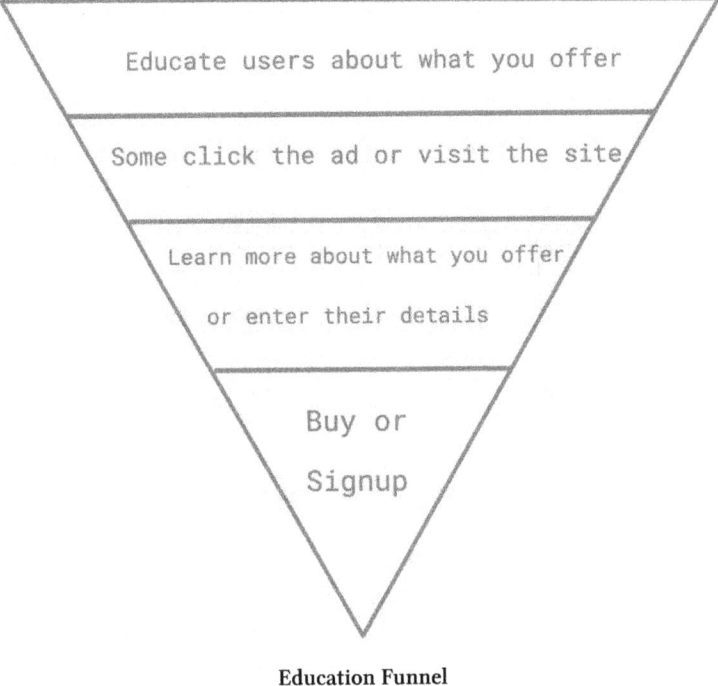

Education Funnel

How to reach them

For reaching people online, there are several techniques we can use in order to reach our customer personas.

Cold Audiences

The first way that you can target potential customers is through trying to find them as a **cold audience.*** *A cold audience is an audience that you target that had no previous interaction with you, so they are *cold* in that they don't have an opinion about your product or service. As a general rule, cold audiences typically have a lower conversion rate (the percentage of them that turn into customers are lower), as opposed to a **warm audience** (anyone that previously visited your website / app, or you have positively interacted with in the past).

A cold audience can be reached in a **behavioral** or a **contextual** way, or a combination of any of the methods listed below.

Behavioral Targeting: This targeting method has to do with the user themselves. In behavioral targeting, you target users based on data you gather, which is either:

1. Information gathered about them online

or

2. Their browsing and interaction behavior

Demographics: The first way that you can target online is based on demographics. In the context of digital marketing, demographics are user data that is mostly gathered from information a user inserts themselves online. For example, when a user signs up for a social media account, they are asked basic questions such as their birthday, where they live, where they studied, where they work, their job title, their relationship status etc. This data can be used by advertisers to target specific people that fit under their preferred target demographic. Demographic target usually is very accurate because it is information that the user volunteers themselves.

Interests: Another way you can target people is based on their interests. This can be guessed about users online by looking at their browsing behavior and in the context of social media, the kinds of pages and people they follow. For example, if I like Football, I'll probably frequent pages that mention football scores from the latest matches and follow sports commentators and famous athletes. Of course, this is not 100% and there is some margin of error, as I could just follow a page because I'm a fan of the person but not necessarily the sport, but it's a good indication, nonetheless.

Location: The next way in which you can target users is based on their location. Location could be a continent, country, city or neighborhood. You can even use radius targeting, to target the area within a circular radius. This last technique is often used to target users that are in a neighborhood that you think your users live in (such as fancy areas with high net worth individuals). **Behavior**: Users can also be targeted directly based on their behavior. What behavior you can target depends on the platform you're targeting. Usually it is an action that is taken by the user related to the platform they are using. For example, you can target a user that recently moved to a new city through behavior targeting. This is something that can be tracked by the ad platform, because if the user was using a social media app for example, they would track that the user changed their current city.

Contextual Targeting: This targeting method has to do with the content of the websites or apps that users frequent. Instead of targeting users on the basis of their online behavior, you target users based on the content they consumer. For example, instead of targeting users that are interested in Football (which could show the ad on any page a user interested in football goes on), I instead show the ad to a football website (which would show the ad to anyone visiting that particular website).

Social Media Posting Versus Ads

If you're running Push marketing ads through social media channels, one of the most common questions I come across whenever someone gets started with social media ads is: What is the difference between boosting a post and running an ad?

This is a common question because most businesses just start posting normally (organically i.e. without paying), then they "boost" their posts (which the social platforms make it very easy to do).

The short answer is there isn't much of a difference, except that boosting a post is limited in its capability, while running an ad gives you a lot more targeting and planning options (with regards to bids and budgets) than boosting gives you.

Audience Targeting

Besides behavioral and contextual targeting, you can also target users based on audiences you define. Two popular examples of this are:

Audience Matching: With audience matching, I can show my ad to any user whose contact details (email or phone number) I have access to. This is a great way to target potential customers who reached out to you in the past, but have not closed the deal yet, or to remarket to existing customers (to have them purchase again). This method can be used for both push marketing and pull marketing ads (where you only target specific users you define in your audience list). Based on my experience, conservatively around 20% of emails you upload will be matched. So if you have a list of 1,000 emails you upload to Facebook, I would expect a minimum of 200 to be matched for targeting (the reason it can be so low is that people often have multiple emails, and not all of them are linked to all of their online accounts). Audience matching is a great way to target users whose emails you have, if you a) Don't want to spam them with emails and b) Don't want them to know that you have their contact details. It is also widely used in the B2B (business to business) community for sales. How it usually works is that you target your prospective clients with an audience targeted ad, which warms them up to you, because many of them would see the ad, so when your sales team reaches out to them (even if it's a cold call), they would have some prior knowledge of your company offering.

Engagement Audiences: Another way to target users is through engagement audiences, which is an audience you can great based on previous behavior on the platform you're targeting. For example, if a user watches a video on your Facebook page, you can target them with an ad if they watch more than 10 seconds of your video.

This is a great way to drive people down the funnel, since you can show them a video ad, to test their initial interest, and then follow it up with an ad to directly sell to them (with a call to action).

Lookalike Audiences

A great way for you to increase the size of your audience and target more people is to use a feature that is built into many ad platforms, known as **Lookalike audiences**. A lookalike audience is a larger audience that you can create, based on a smaller audience you already have. The way that it works is once you create a lookalike audience, the ad platform looks for similarities in your existing audience, and expands your audience based on the similarities it finds based on machine learning. For example, if you have an audience of 1,000 existing customer emails, you can upload that list to create through audience matching (as listed above). Then you can create a lookalike audience based on that initial list, which will expand your list of 1,000 to give you a new audience list of 50,000 users. The way it expands it, is by looking at dozens of signals and unique attributes of your list. You could be a restaurant selling pizza, and the ad platform through its machine learning notices that 90% of your customers also play golf, so it will expand your audience to other golf players in your area. Lookalike audiences can be very effective (based on my experience they are undoubtedly better than normal cold audiences), however the downside is you don't know exactly what the audience contains (since you are not given access to any of the areas that have been matched or any details on who was matched), so you just have to take the word of the ad platform.

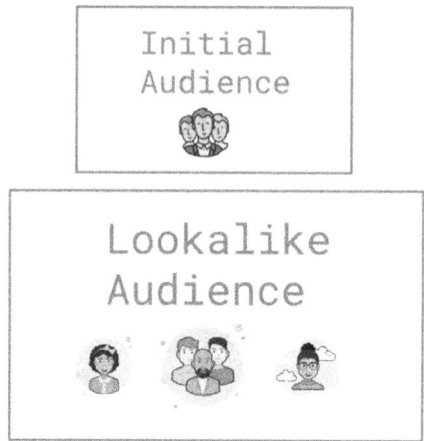

Lookalike Audiences

Retargeting / Remarketing

Once you start running ads, you'll always have a certain percentage of users that come to your website that come close to, but don't actually complete an action (for example adding a product to their online cart but not completing a purchase).

These users can be shown ads again that follow them across the internet to try to get them to complete the desired action. These types of ads are known as retargeting or remarketing ads.

You may be familiar with these ads, as the ads that follow you across the internet after you view a product on a website. Although these ads can seem annoying, if done correctly that can have a huge impact on your overall conversion rate.

```
1) User Visits Website,
   (but doesn't complete desired action)
```

```
2) Audience is created
   (by dropping browser cookie)
```

```
3) Create an ad that remarkets to
   that audience
```

Remarketing

How Retargeting / Remarketing Works

(Since retargeting and remarketing have the same definition in all practical purposes, I'll be using the word remarketing since it's the more widely used catch all term)

The way remarketing works is that first a user visits your website or app and perform an action that you deem desirable but not complete. For example, a user goes to a sales page but doesn't complete a purchase. What you then do is create an audience of users based on that action. This is done by automatically dropping a small file on the user's browser (known as a browser cookie) that tracks that user across the internet. This allows you to follow a user with push marketing display ads.

Remarketing Audience List

The first thing that is required to do remarketing is an audience list. This list is the condition that needs to be satisfied in order for remarketing to take place. Usually it is created based on an action that a user takes on a website (for example, adding a product to a cart, but not checking out). Your remarketing audience list will be auto-populated as soon as a user satisfies the conditions you define.

Connect to ads to follow

Once you create your initial remarketing audience list, the next step is to connect that list to your ad platform. That is done by connecting it to the push marketing channels listed earlier (mainly on Google and Facebook). Once this is done, you can now serve ads to the remarketing audience list and your remarketing campaign will be active.

Conversion Removal

A condition that you want to define in your remarketing campaign is that once a user completes the action you want them to complete, they will no longer see the remarketing ad. For example, if you create a remarketing ad for an eCommerce store based on the users that abandoned their shopping cart, if a user comes back and completes their purchase, you want to make sure they no longer see the ad!

Cookie Window

The beauty of remarketing is that it can be done on a browser basis, which means that a user does not have to be logged into your website or app, for remarketing to work. As long as they have the same browser open and the user did not delete their browser cookies (the files that are temporarily stored on their browser), remarketing will work. Therefore, the next setting you need to define is your cookie window. The cookie window is how long do you want a user to stay on your list (i.e. how long do you want the browser cookie to be active). By default, this is set to 30 days, but you can shorten or lengthen this depending on your product.

Frequency Cap

The final area you can optimize for is your frequency cap for the remarketing ads you're running. The frequency cap is the number of times you want to show your remarketing ad to a single user in a certain time period. For example, you can set this to be x number of times per day, per week or per month. Based on campaigns I've run, I usually set the frequency cap for remarketing campaigns to be 3 times a week if I'm being conservative, and 3 or more times a day if I'm trying very hard to push a sale.

Let me give you some practical examples of the 2 main ways that remarketing works on Google and Facebook.

Example on Google

1. Make sure Google Analytics is installed on your website
2. Create your remarketing audience list through Google Analytics with your desired conditions
3. Link your Google Analytics Audience to your Google Ads account
4. Create a remarketing ad on Google Ads with the audience you imported

This can also be accomplished by adding the Google ads pixel to your website; using the Google Analytics method above, however, is easier to get started with.

Example on Facebook

1. Install the Facebook pixel on your website
2. Create your remarketing audience list through Facebook ad manager with your desired conditions
3. Create a remarketing ad on Google Ads with the audience you imported

Dynamic Remarketing Ads

If you have a lot of products or pages that you'd like to have remarketed, instead of creating an audience for each variation, you can have a dynamic audience created for each product. This is especially useful if you are constantly changing your inventory (in the case of an eCommerce company for example).

The way this works is the same as mentioned above, the only difference is that instead of manually creating your audiences, you create a **product feed**, which is a list of all of your products, from which your audiences will be automatically created.

Paid Remarketing Services

Another option for remarketing is to use a paid service that manages the entire process for you. This is easier to set up and allows you to create holistic campaigns that simultaneously run across all channels. However, it is more expensive than running them on your own (since these services usually either have fixed charges or charge you on a per sale basis).

Targeting your new audience with ads

Let's get back to how we can target a new customer persona with ads. For push marketing, we can target them directly based on the customer persona we define. Depending on the platform, this can either be done by targeting the content (as is the case with the Google Display Network), or the demographic data of the user (as is mainly the case with social media channels, like Facebook, Instagram etc.) In the case of targeting based on content, we need to think about what kind of websites would our target customers go to? This can be guessed by thinking about their likes and dislikes that you defined earlier. For example, if you know that your customers are interested in event management, you can choose to target websites, blogs, or videos on YouTube that talk about events (or events in their city). This way of targeting the content that the user consumes is a good way to get in front of them.

The other way to reach these people is by targeting them based on their interests or directly based on their demographics. The way you would do this is different for every platform, but the common method is that you define either "Interests" which is based on browsing behaviour and pages / people they follow, "Demographics", which is based on information a user inputs in their profile, like location, marital status, educational status, and employment history, or "Behaviour" which are things that a user has done in the past, such as using a type of phone, or making an online payment.

For pull marketing, the trick is that you want to be seen by people that would be searching for your product or service. That is easy enough whenever you have something that someone is already searching for. For example, if I was an airline selling tickets, I can show an ad to anyone searching for "flights to London", and that would be relevant to them, because they are looking for airline tickets. That's the best-case scenario. Unfortunately, though, you don't always get people that are directly searching for what you want to offer.

So, what do you do if you want to use Pull Marketing to people that are not searching directly for you? In that case you can meet people halfway. What I mean by that is that you want to show your ads to people that are searching for something that you offer, but not in a direct way by convincing them that what you offer solves the problem they were searching for. For example, if you were selling summer dresses, instead of showing your ad to someone who is searching for summer dresses, you could show your ad to people that are searching for "summer fashion trends" or "how to look cool this summer", anything that you feel your product or service would solve.

Another way to reach people through this channel, is to show your ads to tangentially related searched. This would generally have a lower response rate (click through rate), but it can be a useful tactic if what you offer is not being searched for. Continuing with the summer dresses example, we can target words like "fashion trends", "mall discounts", "summer sales" etc. This is risky as it can waste money, but it may get results depending on the business.

Testing different profiles

Now that you have an idea of the strategies for targeting your customer profiles, the trick now is to see if your assumptions are correct. Are your customers mainly female? Do they like to go out on the weekend? Are they interested in interpretive dance? Whatever the assumptions are that you have for your customer profile are, you need to test them and see if they actually hold up.

The main questions I would try to answer are:

1) What are their demographics?

Gender, Location, Age, Marital Status, Do they have kids, Employment Status, Educational Status etc.

2) What do they enjoy doing (their likes)?

3) What do they NOT like doing (their dislikes)?

Both of these answers could be generic, or could be tied to what you're selling. So for example if you're selling sports clothing ,you could think directly about your customer's likes or dislikes in a generic way, like how they're working class people above the age of 25, or if you want to be more specific to what you're selling, you would have likes be related to how they're interested in a hobby like basketball for example.

4) How can your product improve their lives?

A more advanced way of doing this is, thinking about how your product can improve their lives. This may seem high level, but it can be really effective in helping you think about the actual value you bring. Starting with the value or "why" they should care (as Simon Sinek famously mentions in his "Start with Why" philosophy) allows you to drive at the root of the pain you're trying to solve, or the gain you're trying to introduce into their lives. People respond much better when you can relate how a product or service can impact their lives, as opposed to keeping things abstract, or focuses on its uses. For example, if I were to think about our eCommerce example, instead of just thinking about the type of product I'm selling (mentioning the selling points), I could think about how it would improve their lives (mentioning the value). So, for a T shirt, instead of mentioning how this is a medium sized blue shirt, I'll focus on how you can look and feel great this summer. The shirt is the means, but the goal is the why behind it. Focusing on why something is important to your customers is the best way to get them to engage. Show them the value.

Pull Marketing

Focus on your products / services

For pull marketing ads, particularly for Google search, the easiest way to get started with ads is just to start targeting the products and services you sell. This could be the brand name of products, for example if you're selling laptops, you could target the keyword "MacBook Air 13 inch", or it could be the product or service itself, such as "laptops".

Generic Keywords

When you are running ads for keywords people search for that are not tied to your company brand name, those are known as **generic** keywords (such as the two laptop examples listed above). Generic keywords are usually where you will face the most growth.

Brand Keywords

When you run ads targeting your brand name (your company name) on ads, these are known as **brand keywords**. For example, if your company is called "Adam's Tea Shop", then you'll target "Adam's Tea Shop" (and the different variations of it), in your ads.

You may be wondering why you need to do this, since shouldn't the search engine already rank your brand name organically? Well there are 3 main reasons why when you do a search for your brand name on a search engine (let's take Google as the example), you might not see your company be in the first position.

1) There may be others: The first reason why you may need to target your brand name is there may be others with the same company name. If there are 3 shops named "Adam's Tea Shop", you'll have a harder time being number one on Google.

2) You maybe new: If you just launched your website, the search engine might need time to rank your brand name, so you may need to wait a while under you appear (see the next chapter on how to speed up this process).

3) You may have technical issues: Your site may have technical issues that prevent you from appearing in the search engine (we also lay out the problems and how to solve them in the next chapter).

4) You may have competitors: An area for which search engines are often criticized is they allow anyone to show their ad on any keywords. This means that any competitor can show their ad on any brand keyword. For example, Pepsi could show their ads to people searching for "Coca Cola". Of course, you'll have to pay more (because your quality score will be lower), but anyone can bid on any keyword. Therefore, if you have a competitor that is running Google Search Ads on your brand name, it will show their website first, and then in the organic results, unless you also create an ad that targets your brand name (in which case 99% of the time you'll be number 1, because you'll have a perfect quality score for your brand name).

Focusing on competitors

So, when should you focus on competitors? It's a risky move, because if you bid on your competitors brand keywords, they may also start bidding on yours, so it's a risk you'll have to calculate by looking at their search volume and their CPC, to see if it's beneficial for you.

Focus on the long tail

Do you know what percentage of online searches are more than 3 words long? Over 70%!

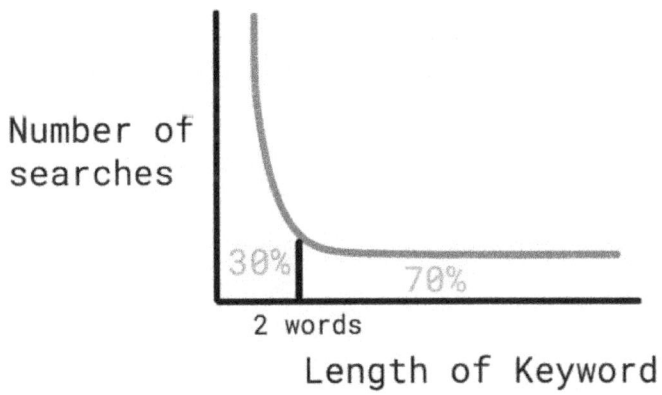

Long Tail Searches

Another area that can be used to target people who are searching on Google is to only show your ad to "long tail keywords". A long tail keyword is usually defined as searches that are at least 3 words long. So, for example someone searching for "buy mens blue t shirt size medium". That search, which may not be very common (it probably only gets a dozen or so searches per month in any given large city), is very specific and shows intention to buy. A good strategy is to have as many of these keywords as you can find, since although individually these types of keywords don't get a lot of searches, combined together they will give you a substantial amount of relevant traffic if done right.

Focusing on Behavior for Search

Instead of directly targeting searches that are directly related to your product, you can also think about what the behaviour or searches of your potential customers are. For example, if you are selling skin care products, instead of targeting keywords like "skin care products", you can instead try keywords like "how to have better skin".

Another classic creative example of this that was done well is Snickers targeting common words people type that had misspellings in them. Then they showed them a funny ad saying, "You can't spell properly when you're hungry", and took them to a Snickers promotion page.

Funny Search Example

This way of doing targeting is risky though, as they had to spend a lot of money, since they had very low-quality scores on those words (since the searches weren't directly tied to their business). It doesn't have to be that extreme though. Another example of this is if you're selling shoes, you could show your Google search ad to people that are searching for "walking distance to certain location", then target them with an ad to tell them about your comfortable walking shoes.

Doubling down or testing other assumptions

Once you try marketing to different demographics, you'll either get good results or you won't. If you do get good results, then double down on what's working and further refine your customer personas. If you don't get good results, then further refine your customer persona and test other assumptions.

Action Plan

1. Build Your Customer Persona. How would you describe who the people you're targeting are?
2. How will you reach them? Define the kinds of:

   a. Interests and things they dislike
   b. What websites or apps do they use
   c. What do they search for online?

3. Choose the generic and brand keywords you want to target with your ads (including long tail keywords)
4. Start running your first campaigns for Push marketing and Pull marketing

Chapter 6 - Getting Free Traffic

The best things in life are free, or so I've heard. Everyone loves free traffic. In a perfect world you would just build it and they would they would come. In a perfect world, you wouldn't have to spend any money on marketing at all (and you wouldn't need to read this book), but unfortunately life isn't perfect. Luckily with Digital Marketing, there are a lot of ways for you to get traffic 100% free! Well, maybe free in terms of money, but you have to pay with another currency: **time**.

These techniques I'll be discussing in this chapter, are ones that you need to invest a lot of time in, if you want them to work. If you do get them working though, they can do wonders in building you consistent very low cost and yes more than often even free traffic. The disadvantage of this strategy is again, that it takes time. If you need quick results, or if you want to amplify your long-term efforts, I suggest you implement the techniques mentioned in the last chapter. In this chapter, we're going to be going over the ways in which you can get free (or very low cost) traffic in a sustained way through a **long-term marketing strategy**.

Long Term Marketing Strategy

This next strategy is one that goes by many names. Some people call it "Content Marketing", "Growth Hacking", "Bootstrapped marketing" or "Inbound marketing". All of these terms work, but for me, I like to call it **Long Term Marketing**, since it focuses on long term sustainable winds, while at the same time not costing very much.

Instead of paying with ads, instead you pay with your time, by thinking of ways to drive traffic to your site and optimizing that traffic for conversions. It's a growth strategy where you focus on optimizing your entire system and conversion funnel in a long term and sustainable way. This involves not spending much money on ads, but instead focus on:

- Generating content in the form of blogs, videos and podcasts

- Getting as many emails as you can into your funnel by having lead magnets, giveaways and competitions to get more people onto your list

- Focusing on platforms that bring you organic (free) traffic, like social media sites, content aggregator sites and sites within your niche

- Running offline events and efforts to get more people into your funnel

- Focus on free PR to get the word out

Let's now dive into the main ways you can build a strategy through long term marketing.

Search Engine Optimization (SEO)

Do you know what the most popular website in the world is? If you answered **Google**, you'd be correct. Even in countries where Google is not the most popular search engine (like in China with Baidu, and Russia with Yandex), some form of search engines is always the most popular site, and usually the homepage that users first go on when they browse the internet. The first channel we're going to focus on for long term marketing is SEO or Search Engine Optimization, which is the strategy you can use to get organic (free) traffic from search engines by optimizing a areas that we're going to discuss in detail.

SEO is a very complicated field. It is a very sought-after specialized career, and one that takes years to master. What I'm going to give you in this section are the highlights and principles that govern SEO that remain constant.

How Search Engines Work

The first thing you should know is that when you do a search on a search engine you aren't actually searching the internet. What is actually happening is you are searching the computers (or servers) of whatever website you are on. For example, if I search for "flights to paris" on Google, Google doesn't actually search the internet for flights to paris. Instead what it does is search its own computers (or servers) for all mentioned of websites that contain those words. The key reasons you need to understand this are:

1. If your website is not on Google (or any other search engines) servers, people can't find it when they do a search.
2. The process by which you get your website to be stored in the Search engine servers is called **indexing**
3. **Indexing** is usually done automatically through software called spiders. For example, Google sends out these software spiders to **crawl** (search) the internet for new websites
4. It is possible for the **index** to not properly **crawl** your website. That will result in your website not being shown on the search engine!
5. If it's on the index, your job is not done, you still need to **rank** high (preferably on the first page) of search results. This is mostly done through content and link building (which we'll discuss in more detail later in this chapter).

The process by which you need to optimize these areas of your website can be summarized in the following 4 areas of the pyramid (which we mentioned briefly in chapter 2).

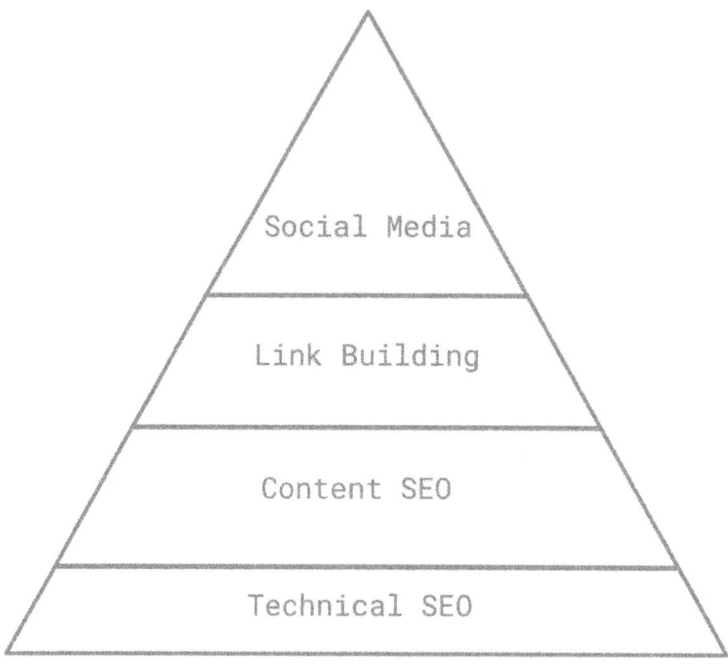

SEO Pyramid

It's in the form of a pyramid, because you need to start with the bottom first, and then move your way up (otherwise you won't have a strong foundation to build on). I'm going to be focusing on Google for the rest of this chapter, but these principles apply to any search engine.

Technical SEO

The first area you need to focus on is Technical SEO, which entails making sure that your website is properly indexed, crawled and ranked by the search engine. It is our starting point, since if you are not indexed by the search engine, nothing else matters!

Checking how your site ranks

The first thing you can do to see how your site ranks is to go onto the search engine. There is a command you can use to check how many pages are in the index.

For Google, this command is: **site:yourdomain.com**

For example, if I want to see how many pages for the AstroLabs website are, I can type the command into Google: **site:astrolabs.com**, and at the time of writing this book, I can see that there are 3,790 pages.

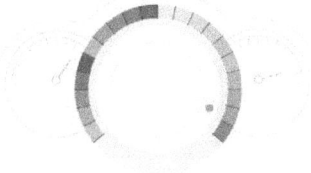

Google Search Console

How can you use this information? The main way is for you to see how many pages Google has in its index, versus how many pages your website actually has (which you can check from your website backend or from Google Analytics). If you notice a big difference in these numbers (the amount you find by writing that command versus the pages you know you have), then there is most likely a problem with the indexing of your website.

Webmaster Tools

The first thing you need to setup when it comes to SEO for your website, is to sign up for something called Webmaster Tools (for

Google this was recently rebranded to "Search Console").

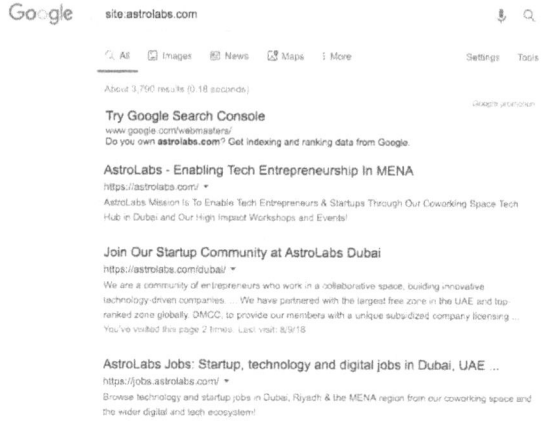

Searching for your site

This is a free tool that every Search Engine (Google, Bing, Baidu etc.) has that allows you to:

1. See if there are any indexing or other errors the Search Engine noticed on your site
2. Track top performing SEO searches
3. Have a direct communication channel with the Search Engine.

The last point is actually one of the most important ones, since it allows you to talk to the Search Engine directly and submit pages to be indexed if you notice anything is missing.

The files to look out for

Once you have Webmaster tools setup, you need to make sure that there are 2 files in particular on your website are properly implemented. This is usually something that is done by your developer (or the technical person on your team). The 2 files you need to properly setup are:

Robots.txt: This is the first site that a search engine "crawls" or reads when it comes to your website. The purpose of this file is to:

a) Let the search engine know if there are any pages you do NOT want to have indexed. For example, if there are any private pages on your website, or temporary pages that you don't want the public to find out about if they do a search.

b) Point to the next file, which is the Sitemap file.

Sitemap.xml: This is the most important file to have implemented on your website, when it comes to the pages that are being indexed. This file lets the search engine know about **all** of the pages that you want to have indexed (stored for users to find when they do a search). You may be asking, why do I even need such a file? Doesn't the search engine automatically read or "crawl" the internet for new pages? Why do I have to explicitly tell it the pages I want to have indexed? Well the short answer is that, a Search engine might miss some pages. Examples of this could be:

- a. You recently added a lot of pages and the search engine didn't have a chance to index them all yet
- b. You have some pages that are not linked from other pages (i.e. orphan pages), which make it hard for the search engine to find them.

Once you have those 2 files, you shouldn't have any indexing problems. In fact, if you have your **Sitemap.xml** file, you can actually submit it to the search engine (through your Webmaster tools login), which would cause the search engine to come back and re-index your pages. In other words, it's a direct connection for you to talk to Google (or any of the other search engines)!

Duplicate content

The next area you need to worry about when it comes to Technical SEO is duplicate content. According to Google, between 25-30% of the web has duplicated content (content that is posted more than once). In order to combat this, search engines penalize content that is viewed as duplicated. For example, if CNN or BBC writes a new article and I copy it word for word and post it on my own blog, I most likely will not appear in the search engine for that content, because now it's smart enough to know if content is duplicated.

It's not just about copying from other sources. Even if you copy from yourself, you could be penalized. For example, if you're a company that has websites in multiple countries, if you duplicate content across your website, you'll notice that some of your pages won't appear properly in search engines.

301 redirects

The easiest way to solve duplicate content problems is to remove the duplicate and just point to the old version. This is only a solution though, if you want to get rid of one of the versions. For example, if you have a new version and an old version of your website, you can add a redirect (in technical terms this is called a 301 redirect), which will automatically redirect the old version of the page to the new version.

Canonical links

If you want to keep both versions, the other solution is to "cite your source" and keep both versions. This is just like how in university if you wrote a paper you would need to have a reference section. For SEO, this is called a **canonical link**. So, for example, if I copy an article from one section of my website to another,

I can add a canonical link in the copied version, that points to the original version. Although this is a good solution, the problem with it though, is it automatically means that you need to choose a "preferred" or "original" version of the content, since whatever you choose as the original version will get most of the ranking benefits.

Localization tags

The last solution you can employ, is to add a localization tag to your code. This is something that when added, will tell the search engine that if a user is in that geography (or is browsing in a certain language), that you prefer to serve them a variation of that content. It is done by adding the below code to your page.

<link rel="alternate" hreflang="*lang_code*"... >

For example, if I have three versions of my site, one in English for the UK, one in English for the US, and one in French for France, I can add a tag on each of the page versions to specify to the search engine, which version of the site I want to serve, depending on where the user is.

What makes content duplicated?

The question people often ask is, how much content is it ok to copy? From what I've seen, it's difficult to give a hard cut-off point, but my general rule of thumb is if I'm copying content that is more than a paragraph (a few sentences), then I would rewrite it.

Page Speed / Mobile

The final top area that I recommend you focus on for technical SEO is to make sure that your site loads fast and is mobile optimized (meaning that it looks good on smaller screens). Quick site loading can usually be accomplished by optimizing images (saving them in smaller file formats), using **caching** (saving data in the users browsers so it loads faster the next time they visit the site), and using a **CDN** (content delivery network), which is a service you can subscribe to that loads your large size items (like images) from geographies close users. Mobile optimization can be accomplished by making your site **responsive**, which means it will auto resize based on the screen size.

Content SEO

The second level of the pyramid is to focus on content. If technical SEO is the foundation of your building, content is the actual building itself. It's actually the most important thing you can optimize, since it's what gets picked up by the search engine algorithm, when it determines where to show your site, based on the keywords that a user types into the search engine.

Identifying keywords

The first step to ranking for words on SEO is figuring out what words you want to rank for! That means you need to combine three things:

1) What products / services your site offers: This is the most obvious way, just by directly choosing what you're selling. For example, if you're selling blue t-shirts, then you target the word "blue t-shirts".

2) What you think people are searching for related to your business: This is where you have to use some personal judgement and come up with words and phrases that make sense to you, that you think people would search for. For example, if you're selling clothes you might think people would look for "best t-shirts", "best price on t-shirts" etc. Your guesses at this stage could be right or wrong, but it's important that you do some brainstorming at this stage.

3) See what people are actually searching for: The last stage is to check your assumptions and see what people are actually searching for. The main way of doing this is by using a keyword research tool. These are the tools that are used to track behaviour of people online. For example, if you use the Google Keyword Planner tool (a tool you can use for free by creating a Google Ads account), you can search for any topic like "t-shirts", and it will tell you what are the most common searches for people that search for related keywords in the geography that you chose. The main reason it's useful to use a keyword research tool is that you don't know what people are actually searching for. Are people searching for "t-shirts" with a dash, or "t shirts" without a dash? You can never know unless you actually look at the data. Another interesting fact is that according to Google, on any given day 15% of all searches have never been done before in history! That's because every day there are new words and phrases people use, new cultural references, and new ideas. You can never guess people's behavior online, unless you look at the data!

Placing keywords

Once you identify the keywords that you want to target, the next step is to figure out where to place them on the page so you can rank for those words. This exercise is done on a per page basis. So that means that ideally, you should target between 1-5 keywords per page that you want to rank for and put them in the following places.

I'll keep this section short and sweet. There are 6 main sections you need to put keywords that you want to rank for. They are:

Content of the page: This is the actual body of the page. You should place any keywords you want to rank for somewhere on the page. The more times you mention a keyword the better (you should try to mention it at least a couple of times somewhere on the page). However, you need to make sure that it is natural and flows with the content of the page. Do not try to insert a keyword on a page more times than makes sense. The practice of adding a keyword too many times unnaturally on the page is known as **keyword stuffing** and doing so is penalized by the search engine if detected.

Page title: The next area to place a keyword you want to rank for is it put it in the page title. This is not actually seen on the page by the user but is instead seen in two places a) On the tab of the browser and b) On the SERP (search engine results page).

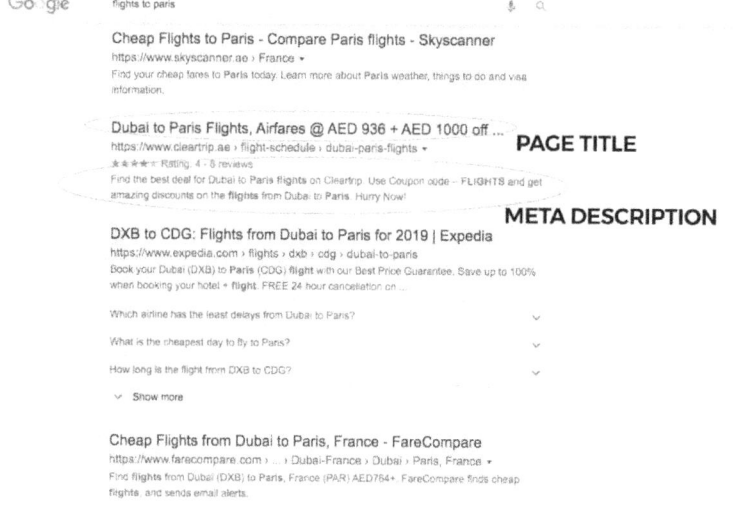

Search Engine Results Page

Meta Description: The next area you need to place your keywords in, are in the meta description. This is only seen on the SERP. This is the one place on this list that doesn't have a direct impact on your ranking. However, if you place a keyword in the meta description, it will cause it to appear bolded whenever someone searches for that word, which although it doesn't have a direct impact on ranking, improves your CTR (click through rate), or how many people click on your ad. Fun fact: An average user spends only about 5 seconds on a Google search before they click on a result! That means tiny improvements in your Page title and meta description can have a big difference.

Header (H1): This is the header text that you see on the page (as opposed to the page title which is not actually seen on the content of the website). It is probably the most overlooked of all of the places to insert a keyword, since people don't realize the importance of it. From a technical or coding point of view, it is essential that this has the <h1> label, since that's what the search engine looks for when it classifies that page. If you have a page slider on top of your website, then you can have the slider text be the <h1> text.

H1 Example

Image titles and alt descriptions: The next place to insert the keywords you want to rank for are on your images. This needs to be updated in two places. a) The image title: For example, don't call your image "imageversion2.jpg", but instead call it something that describes it like "blue_t-shirt.jpg" b) The image "alt" description: This is another one of the places that the user doesn't actually see, but it's implemented in the code and is used for ranking. The point of the alt description tag for images is so make your site accessible to people with disabilities (for example, if someone is blind and has your site read to them). Therefore, the alt description tag should be added to all of your images in such a way that it describes the image in vivid detail. For example, you could say something like "Blue T-Shirt with an open collar".

URL: The next place where you can add the keyword is in the URL of the page. This is one that you cannot always implement, since sometimes you don't have any power to change the URL (for example on the homepage of your website). If you can change the URL though, then it is recommended that you do. For example, if you have a product page for a blue t-shirt, don't call the URL "yoursite.com/product-123sdaf", but instead name it something logical with the keyword you want to target like "yoursite.com/product/blue-t-shirt". For search engines, when you insert anything in the URL, since you can't have a space you add a "-", which takes the search engine interprets as a space.

Tracking keywords

Once you put the keywords in the places I mentioned above on your website, the next step is to track them. There are 2 ways to do this. 1) **By using data from Webmaster tools:** The webmaster tools setup I mentioned earlier gives you minimum insight into how your top keywords are doing, but it doesn't paint a full picture. 2) **Using a keyword tracker:** If you want to get a full picture of how you rank for your target keywords over time, you need to use some kind of **keywords tracker** (I'll mention some of the ones I recommend in the appendix of this book).

Link Building

The next level of the pyramid is to focus on **link building**. Link building is the process of getting other websites to create a link that would send users to your website if they click on it. These are also known as **outbound links**. Outbound links are a major source of ranking on all major search engines.

How it works

One of the reasons that made Google become the market leader in the search engine industry in the late 90's was its implementation of links as a ranking factor. Before Google came up with this idea, search engines only looked at the content of the page. After Google's patented **Page Rank** algorithm came onto the market, suddenly the number of links that point to a website started to make a different. In a way it functions like a vote. So, for example, if your website has a lot of links pointing towards it, it's like all of those other websites are voting that your website is trustworthy, which causes it to rank higher in the search engine.

Link Juice

All links are not created equal. If a get a link from a popular website, it could propel you a lot higher in the search results than a link than a link from a site that is not very popular. For example, if you get one link from CNN, that could boost your ranking quite a bit, but if you get a link from a random small blog, you might barely notice a difference. In the SEO industry, this is known as a website's **link juice**. There is not an actual standard that measures this, but there are some tools that try to estimate the "power" of a link (I list the most popular ones in the appendix).

Typically, the types of websites that have the most popular types of links are:

Government websites (ending in .gov)Educational website (ending in .edu)News websites (CNN, BBC, Huffington Post, Buzzfeed etc.)

Link Trading

One of the areas that you need to be careful from in SEO, is you want to avoid **trading links**. Let's say website A links to website B. Website B will get a boost in their ranking because they received a link from website A. However, if website B then links back to website A (let's say mentioning them in their press section) the links would cancel out in the eyes of the search engine! They would still function normally for the user, but the ranking benefits would no longer be in effect for website B. The reason this is the case, is because search engines want to discourage people from trading links in a nefarious way that messes with the algorithm.

Result: Links cancel each other

Link Trading

No Follow Links

Let's say you want to link back to someone's website that already linked to you but you want to avoid the above scenario. Luckily, there is a way to tag your links to avoid the trading links penalty. The way to do this is to add a **no follow** link tag in the code of your link.

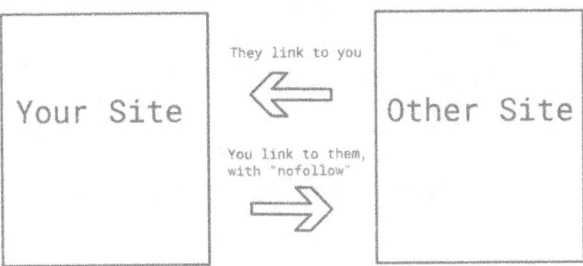

Result: You get an SEO Boost

No Follow Link

By adding a no follow link to your link, the search engine will ignore it in its ranking algorithm. It will still function like a normal link, but you will avoid any penalties that may have been caused as a result of trading links.

Social Media Links for SEO

One of the things you might be thinking is, ok why not start posting my links on social media? Social media sites are super popular, and they should give me a lot of link juice and ranking benefits if I post them there, right? While that sounds good in theory, unfortunately, social media links have no clout in the SEO world. All links that you post on social media posts are classified as **no follow** links. Why is this the case? Mainly to avoid users posting too much spam (since if social media sites allowed links to count for SEO rankings, there'd be a lot more spam links and that would ruin the user experience).

So, is posting links on social media still worth it? Of course! Even though links posted on social media sites won't have a direct effect on rankings, it will still get you some traffic, and the spill over effect will help with your SEO (just not in a direct way).

Link Building Ideas

Now that you know the importance of getting links pointed towards your site, how do you go about getting links? This process in the SEO world is known as **link building**, and there are a few popular techniques you should implement.

Generate Great Content

The best most sustainable way to do long term link building is to just generate great content! That means mainly, having your own blog where you post your own useful valuable content that people want to share. By posting great content, people will start sharing it on social media (which will have a spill over effect), you'll get organic traffic SEO, and if anyone references your post in their own blog or articles, that will give you a direct SEO boost. What kind of content should you post? The main way I found is to answer questions you think people may have. If you're selling t-shirt, write a blog post on the best ways to find a shirt that fits you. If you're selling laptops, write posts on how to choose the best laptops etc. Whatever you think your customers would be interested in, and that you see people are searching for (as we mentioned in the content section), write about that!

Video or Podcasts

It doesn't have to just be written either, you might want to create your own vlog, or podcast. What's great about vlogs and podcasts is they allow you to include links in the video or show descriptions, which helps in your link building efforts.

Press / PR

One of the most effective ways to get links (especially those with strong **link juice**) is to get mentioned in press articles online or on news sites. Of course, it helps if you or the company you work for has an angle a reporter can write an interesting story about.

If you have already been mentioned or interviewed in a news article and they didn't include a link to your site, you can reach out and ask them to include a link (I found that about half the time you ask, they'll agree to include a link to your site).

If you're still new and want to get started with this, there are no shortcuts I'm afraid. You just have to do traditional reach out (public relations), reach out to reporters, news publications and magazines until you find someone that wants to write about what you're doing.

Guest Blogging

An easy way to get links is to write your own articles! Most smaller publications online (blogs or smaller news sites) are starving for content, and they'll easily agree for you to write articles for them in your area of expertise. This process is known as **guest blogging**, and it's an old but still effective way for you to generate links to your site. Usually how it works is that you write a free article for another website, which gives them content they can use, and in exchange, you insert a link in the article or in the bio section of the article that links back to your site.

Answer Websites

Another way for you to get links is to answer questions on question and answer sites (like Quora or Reddit), or on forums that are within your niche. As long as you're not spammy in how you answer, it's an effective way to generate links to your site. This can be done by putting links in your answer (if someone asks about where to find x, and if you offer x for example), or it can be unrelated and you just mention in your bio or signature that you work at Company X and have a link to your site there.

Look in your niche

You can also dig into websites that are specific to the niche you are in to look for link building opportunities. For example, if you're in the party planning business, you can find websites that list the best party planning suppliers. If you're a website that offers childcare, you can list your website on mom groups in your city. Sometimes you have to get creative and see where people in your niche and geography are hanging out online.

Use Your Network

Finally, I recommend that you use your network as much as possible. That includes your family and friends (if anyone has their own blogs or websites), your alumni network (posting on your university alumni newsletter for example), or any other groups you're a part of.

Social Media with SEO

The final step of the SEO pyramid is social media. As I mentioned, social media links on SEO are tagged as **no follow** links, so any links that are posted here will not have a direct impact on your SEO ranking (that's why we're talking about social media last for SEO last).

However, even though social media doesn't have a direct impact on ranking for SEO, it is still a useful channel to take advantage of. A few ways social media can help are:

Getting you traffic

Social media is where most people spend their recreational time, so the more you post here the better. At the end of the day, you want you site to get more popular, and where traffic comes from shouldn't be as big of a concern. One way you want to do this is to make it easy for people to share your content. Having a simple share button can make a big difference, since most people, even if they find something interesting on your site, would be too lazy to copy and paste the link.

Social Profiles in the SERP

Another area where social media can help with SEO is by having your brand name take up more space on the SERP (search engine results page) by showing your social profiles (which naturally will bring you more traffic).

Google My Business

If you have a physical address, it is crucial that you list yourself on Google maps and open a **Google My Business** account. This is a free service that will show a map and **knowledge graph** if anyone searches for your brand name, which takes up a lot of space on the search engine.

Organic Social Media

Let's now talk about organic (free) social media. This is different from what was mentioned in the push marketing section of this book in that the following techniques are free, and don't require any money. In practice though, most businesses employ a combination of paid and free tactics when dealing with social media.

Social media is hard for businesses. Did you know on social media when you post something as a company on Facebook for example (in 2019), your reach (how many people will actually see it) is less than 1%? So that means that in theory if you have 1,000 followers and you post something organically (without paying to boost it) on social media, you'll be lucky if 20 people see it!

So how can you get people engaged and interested in your content without paying? The answer is to **provide value** and **have conversations.**

Providing Value

When you're posting on social media, it's important to remember the context. Most people are not on social media to follow brands! So automatically, you're at a disadvantage when you're posting on behalf of your company. The way to get around this is to provide value and not make it about you, but instead show how you can help people in their own lives. What you need to think about, is how can you post things valuable things for your users. That means giving insight into your industry and sharing things that people can use in their lives, not just constantly posting about the products and services you offer. This holistic approach is often known as a **content strategy**, since you need to plan out what are the types of content that you want to post on behalf of your company. Some examples of this could include:

- Facts from your industry / company
- Blog posts, articles, and videos
- Infographics
- Event recaps
- Photos from your company (could be fun photos from your office, or an office event)
- Any knowledge or information you can share

Post where they are!

One of the simplest, yet most effective things you can do when posting your content is to post it where they are. You will get a lot more engagement with your posts if you keep people on the platform where the post is. For example, it is better to summarize an article on LinkedIn than to always redirect people off of LinkedIn to go to your blog.

Batching your content

Another thing you can do is **batch** or **schedule** your content. What that means is that you plan out your content days or weeks in advance to have it take up less time. There are many social media scheduling tools that make it easy for you to do this. For example, you could plan all of your posts at the beginning of the week and schedule them to automatically go out, so you don't have to post manually every day.

Having conversations

Why are most people on social media? It has to do with the **social** part. Humans are social creatures and crave human interaction. Therefore, if you want your content on social media to be interactive, you have to make it a conversation. That means not just constantly posting, but also listening to what others are saying, and having it be a two-way interaction.

Social media Active and Reactive

Sometimes on social media, you don't just want to post one-way communication or be reactive if someone responds to you, you should also be active! What that means is that you start your own conversations with people if it's relevant for your brand. For example, if you're a laptop repair company, you can reply to people on social media that are asking "where can I fix my laptop?". You can find these relevant conversations by doing an advanced search for relevant keywords directly on social media sites, or by using a **social media listening tool**.

Focusing on Real time

One of the macro trends on social media is to focus on **real time** posts. This means that you should post more live content (by live streaming) or post on your **social media story** (a video that disappears after 24 hours). These types of posts (at the time of writing this book) get an automatic boost compared to traditional types of posting (normal images and videos), since they are ethereal in their nature and social media platforms want to encourage more of these kinds of posts to keep people engaged.

Start with Why

Something you should keep in mind when posting on social media, is the fact that you want to focus on the "why" of your message. In pop culture, authors like Simon Sinek (in his book "Start with Why") mention the importance of focusing on the "why" in what you do. Let me illustrate how this is relevant to social media.

There are 3 ways you can focus on posting content online.

What: By focusing on "what" the message is, you're basically just stating facts. This is the least effective method. Let's say that you're marketing a new car. Focusing on the "what" would mean that you just mention the cars features in your social media posts. For example, "The new model has leather seats, cruise control, 4-wheel drive etc."

How: By focusing on the "how" of your message, you're diving a little deeper into the mechanics of your product or service. This is a little better than focusing on the "what", but it is still not the most effective way. For example, this would be talking about how the purchase process works and its unique selling points like "It gets 50 miles to the gallon, you can buy it with a 5-year finance plan etc."

Why: By focusing on the "why" of your message, now you're getting into how it makes your customers **feel** and how it **improves**

their lives. You turn the conversation to be, why should they care about you in the first place. For example, you would say "Get your dream car, live the family life you want etc". It's focusing a lot on the end outcomes that your product or service gives them.

By trying to always post in "why" language, you'll find that your posts will get a lot more engagement. Again, this goes back to focusing on what is the value that your product / service provides!

Tone of Voice

When you're posting for a company or a brand on social media, people often fall into one of the following traps. Either they post in their own voice (how they sound on their personal accounts), or they sound very robotic and corporate. The way that you solve this and be consistent in how you're posting is to come up with your **Tone of Voice**. A tone of voice is how your company sounds to people when you're posting, and if you have a consistent tone of voice, then no matter who is posting, your company or brand will sound consistent in their mind.

The way this is done practically is to come up with 3 words that you want to describe your company or brand. This is what will give a basis to come up with a unified voice. These 3 words can be any adjective that you think is positive and describes your brand.

For example, let's say you work for a luxury fashion retailer. You might say your 3 words are "prestigious, elegant and formal". So now when you're posting on social media, you'll keep those three words in mind, and you'll try to be prestigious, elegant and formal when you post (so that means you probably won't use emojis in your posts).

Let's give another example, and say you work for a children's entertainment company. In that case, your 3 words might be "friendly, fun and adventurous". So now when you're posting you'll keep those 3 words in mind, and you'll use language that's slang than in the previous example, and probably also use a lot of emojis.

A fun technique you can use to help you personify your tone of voice is to come up with your dream celebrity spokesperson. Think about (if money was no option), who would you want to be the spokesperson for your brand (someone that embodies the 3 words you chose). Then when you're posting, always think about how that person would have phrased something. It doesn't have to be an actual celebrity either, some companies I worked with chose their spokesperson to be someone on their team or the company founder for example.

Email Newsletters

Emails are a powerful tool. It is the most robust channel out of any of the other channels listed here. Mainly due to:

1. **The History of email**: Email was around for a very long time (in minor use since the 70's and popular use since the early 90's), which to borrow a phrase from Nassim Taleb, means that it follows the "Lindy" effect (a phenomenon where if something has been around for a long time, it's more likely to stick around longer).
2. **Direct access**: Email gives you direct access to your users, which means you have complete control over your list without any third-party intervention (like a social media channel).
3. **Permission-Based**: Email is permission-based, which means that users have to volunteer to be on your list and they can leave at any time by unsubscribing, which makes people a lot more engaged than when they see a random ad online.
4. **Most Popular**: Email is the most popular channel of communication. If I asked a room of 1,000 people if they use any social media channel (Facebook, Instagram etc.) you will always get

a percentage of people that will say no. If I ask them if they use email, I will either get 99% or 100% of people to say yes. That's the power of email.

5. **Most Cost Effective**: If you look at the cost of email, it's very cheap. The only cost is how much you have to pay to send to a large list (which is a fraction of the cost of running ads). Not to mention the fact that once you have an email, it's yours forever to send at a low cost (as long as they stay subscribed).

How email works

The first thing you need to understand about email is how it works. When an email is sent, it goes through 2 stages. This may seem trivial at first, but you'll see in a bit why it's important to understand this concept (especially with relation to how emails end up in the spam filter).

Stage 1 The Sender: The first stage an email goes through is when it's being sent. The sender clicks send, and the email leaves the sender server and goes across the internet to step 2.

Step 2 The Receiver: The second stage an email goes to is the receiver side. When an email is sent from a sender it then goes to the receiver's server where it reaches the receiver's inbox, if it avoids the spam filter (which we'll discuss shortly).

Can't I send for free?

A common question I receive is why can't I send emails for free? Why do I have to pay for an email client? Can't I just use my Gmail or Outlook account to send emails? While that is an option, there are a few reasons why it's usually always a better option to pay a small fee for an email client.

You are limited by most free options. For Gmail this is between 500 and 1,000 emails per day, so that means that if your list is larger than that, you're out of luck. You can't see analytics or tracking data, which means you won't be able to see how many opens and clicks your email got. You can't do advanced triggers. For example, you can't automatically send an email based on how the response was from a previous email. You can't customize the design. You cannot add merge tags (like how you say Hi FirstName) or add multiples images and columns to format the email in a nice way.

The 4 levels of drop off

Even though email is a very effective channel, there are many drop off points in the user journey once an email is sent.

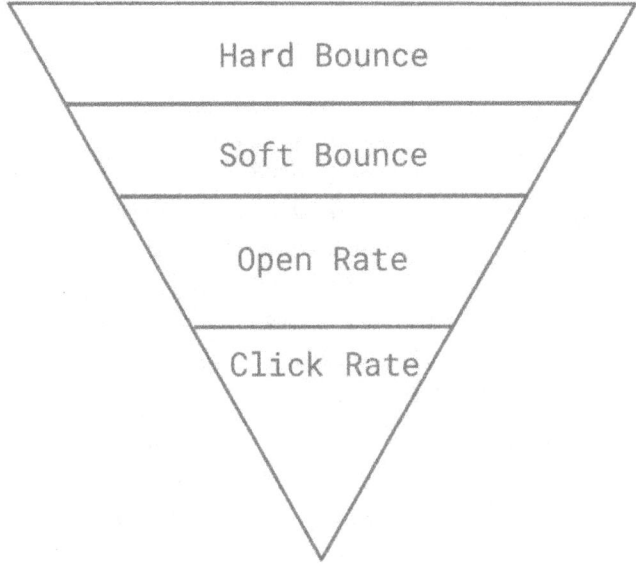

Email Drop Off points

Hard Bounces: If an email is sent but the email address is either not correct or no longer exists, than it cannot be delivered so a hard bounce is registered. A hard bounce can be from someone intentionally or unintentionally writing their email down wrong when they sign up on your website for example. One way this is usually avoided is by having a **double opt in,** which means that when a user signs up, you send them a confirmation email (where they click on the link within the email to confirm their address is valid), before you add them to your list. Most mail clients you will use to send out emails will automatically account for hard bounces (so you don't have to worry about them as much).

Soft Bounces: If the email address is correct, but it doesn't reach the users inbox a soft bounce is registered. A soft bounce can occur if the inbox is full, if it's blocked by the server, or if you're sending a file that's too large. The most common cause of a soft bounce though, is if the email goes to **spam** (we'll discuss in a bit about how to avoid the spam filter).

Open Rate: Once the email reaches the user's inbox, your job is still not done. They still have to open the email! Open rate is the percentage of people that open the email, from the total audience that receives your email. The industry average for open rates are between 20-30%, depending on the business type. So, for example, if you send an email to 1,000 people, on average if your list is in the normal range, you'll probably get between 2,000-3,000 opens (of course the higher the better).

Open rate percentages are never 100% accurate though, since it's calculated by the email client by loading a transparent image that's hidden on the email you send (if the invisible image loads, then it's calculated as an open). This does have some limitations, such as if a user blocks images from loading on their email, or if someone "marks you as read" without opening the email, then it won't count that as an open. The main thing you can change to improve your open rate is to write better **subject lines**.

Click Rate: Once they open your email, you probably want them to take some action, such as buying a product, read your article etc. That means that once they open the email, you probably want them to click on the email and go to your website. The click rate is what is calculated by looking at the total number of clicks you get as a percentage of the total number of people your email was sent to. The industry average for click rate is between 2-4%. So, for example, if you send an email to 1,000 people, on average if your list is in the normal range, you'll probably get between 20-40 clicks.

Avoiding the spam filter

One of the biggest problems that you come across when sending emails is the **spam filter**. This is where the **soft bounces** occur that we mentioned earlier, which occurs when the email doesn't reach the user's inbox. A spam filter is a mechanism that is activated on the side of the receiver that blocks messages from coming in that appear to be spam (not legitimate emails. So, the million-dollar question is, "How do you avoid the spam filter?".

These are my top tips.

Build Trust

To avoid the spam filter, you first have to know how spam works. An email is marked as spam mainly due to one criterion: when it's not seen as trustworthy. If for whatever reason the receiver's email client things you are not trustworthy, you will go to spam.

The way that email spam filters work is they:

1. Look for markers of a spammer. That could be indicators like having a spammy subject line (for example, saying something like "FREE, FREE, FREE!!!"), or sending from a non-validated email or domain (more on that later).
2. They measure the overall trustworthiness of the sender, based on previous behavior.

Did you ever wonder why when you send a normal one-to-one email to someone, you almost never go to spam, but when you send out a mass email, you often do go to spam? That's usually because a normal one-to-one email you send out is by its nature a trustworthy email, because in the past people always open your emails. On The other hand, if you send out a broadcast email to thousands of people, a lot of them might not open the email, so your trust goes down.

So how do you build trust? It's actually a lot like how you build trust for people in real life. You have to be consistent, reliable and honest through good behavior. Let me give an analogy on how email trust works. Let's say that your email trust can be measured as a glass of water. The more water you have, the more trustworthy you are. If you don't have any water in your glass, then you're seen as not trustworthy and go to spam.

Every time you send an email to a person and they open it, your trust goes up. In this example, your glass gets filled with more liquid and you're seen as trustworthy. However, every time you send someone an email and they don't open it, then your trust goes down. That's why you want to make sure that your open rates are consistently high, because the higher they get, the less likely you are to go to spam.

Quality Sender

One of the limitations of email, is that anyone can send an email to anyone else pretending to be someone else. For example, I could send all reading this book an email saying that I am "billgates@microsoft.com". This is due to a limitation within email that allows you to easily fake your sender email. Of course, if you respond back to the email, I won't get the message, because I don't have access to that inbox, but usually hackers use this trick to send you to a different website to steal your information (this is known as a phishing attack).

Because of the ease by which you can fake your email address, most mail clients (like Gmail, Outlook etc.) have a built in mechanism to check for two things:

1. **Is the email validated?**: The first thing that the email client checks for is to see if the email is validated, which means do I (as the sender) have access to that inbox. If we take the previous example, and say I was trying to send you an

email from "billgates@microsoft.com", it would most likely go to spam, because I have no way of validating that email (verifying that I have access to that inbox), unless I am Bill Gates (which unfortunately I can assure you I am not).
2. **Is the domain authenticated?** From a practical point of view, the first thing you need to do to avoid the spam filter is to make sure you're sending emails from a **quality sender**, which means that when someone else gets that email, they are fairly confident that you are who you say you are.

This can be accomplished in two ways. Either:

1. The fast way is for you use a sender that is already high quality. This can usually be done by paying a little extra (I'll mention some that I recommend in the appendix). The disadvantage of this approach, however, is that your emails will be "signed" by that domain. From a practical point of view, this makes little difference, but if a user looks at the details of how the email was sent, they can see that it wasn't sent from your domain. It's also riskier, because you don't have any control if suddenly the sender loses its quality (which could happen).
2. The second more sustainable way it to become a quality sender yourself. The main step this involves is changing some settings in your domain, which are known as the DKIM records. You can Google your email client along with "DKIM setup" to figure out how to do this (this is usually done by your IT team, or the technical person on your team).

Validate what comes in

One of the best ways to prevent your emails going to spam is to make sure people want to be on your list, by being vigilant about who you add to your list. Usually, when someone comes to me telling me that email doesn't work because they have a really bad open rate, it's usually because they are too quick to add people to your list. Think about it. Would you rather have a quality list of 1,000 people that are rabid customers and fans, or 10,000 people that barely know who you are? The first is definitely the better option because you're sure they'll open your emails and help you spread the word organically. More is not always better.

The number one way to validate the emails that come in, is to use a **double opt-in**. A double opt-in is a technique in which you have a user enter their email in a form, then you automatically send them a confirmation email to verify that they want to receive an email from you. This double confirmation is essential to get right because:

1. It is the law in some countries (in parts of the US and the EU especially).
2. It acts as a gate, preventing spammers and people from typing the wrong address in (hard bounces), since if they type the address wrong, they never get a chance to opt-in.
3. It improves your trust, since it forces someone to open an email from you (which is an indication that you are trustworthy). If the person doesn't click the link to confirm they'll never be added to your list. Having a double opt-in may decrease the number of emails you receive, but that basically means that you'll always be left with a quality list of people that (at least initially) want to be there!

Clean list

Another area you want to make sure you keep an eye on, is keeping your list clean! That means you regularly have to purge our emails that are no longer active, or that no longer open your emails. Remember, it's always better to have a smaller active list than a larger inactive one. There are a few ways that I recommend you clean your list:

1. **Use automation:** The first way is to create an automation rule to purge any subscribers that are no longer active. In most email clients you can filter out and delete emails that have not opened, clicked or interacted with you over a certain period of time. For example, you could set up a rule that says that you'll delete a user if they didn't open or click on the last 5 emails you sent them.
2. **Use built in rating:** Most email clients also have a rating system (some give a 1 to 5-star rating) where they rank how engaged an email is. Just regularly clean out the lower ranking emails (including hard bounces, which often times stay in your email list, even though they're inactive and never receive an email).
3. **Use an email scrubbing service:** You could also use an email cleaning or scrubbing service. These are often paid tools that will clean large lists for you by verifying that the emails on your list are active (it does this mainly through behind the scene email server verification).

Write Better Emails

This one may seem obvious, but it needs to be said. You need to write better emails! Write emails that you think your customers would want to open. A good rule of thumb is to think about how you would feel if you received the email you're about to send. Is it just a marketing email that is showing your products in their face, or does it have its own intrinsic value? The more valuable and relevant you make your emails, the more people will want to open them. You could try every trick in the book, but if your emails aren't interesting and useful people will be very unlikely to engage with them.

Consider Going All Text

Think about how you use email on a daily basis. What is the commonality between most of your emails? I can guess that 99.9%

or even 100% of the emails you respond to or all text (they don't contain any images or only minor attachments). That makes sense because that's how we use emails, as a text communication platform. So, it's no wonder that when you send someone an email that contains dozens of images and almost no text, it's no wonder your engagement rate is low.

For some businesses, it makes sense to use nice designs and colorful images. However, for most businesses, if you can, I recommend going back to the roots and core functionality of email in your marketing. Send more personalized text!

Which one looks like a normal you would respond to?

Segmenting and Merge Tags

When you're creating your email list, it's important to remember that there is more information you can gather from the user. That can include things like their name, company, job title, interests, birthdays and more. Whatever data you collect can then be used to either segment your list (put people into groups based on the types of emails you want to send), or to **merge tags**, which is when you use one of the fields you gathered to customize the email (like saying Hi "FirstName"). While this can be a great strategy, keep in mind that if you're requiring a user to fill out a form, the more data you make them fill out, the higher the barrier for them to complete their information is, so it's a balance between getting as much data as you can, to asking too much and turning people away.

Subject Line

If your email doesn't go to spam, the next important thing you need to worry about is if they open the email (which is reflected in the open rate), and the main factor that determines the open rate is the subject line.

The subject line of an email is one of the most important things to optimize, because it's the main variable you can change that has an effect on if the user opens the email or not. It's important to realize that when we talk about **subject line** there are actually 5 main fields that you can optimize when sending out mass emails.

1. **Sender Name:** This is the name of the person or company that's sending the email. This could be the company name (Company X) or if you want to make it more personalized, you could use an actual name of an employee (Sarah from Company X). Based on what I've seen, having the sender name be the name of a person usually gets a higher open rate.
2. **Sender Email:** The next field you can optimize is the sender email, which is what the user sees as the "from" email address. As mentioned earlier, if you want to minimize spam, then you need to make sure that you verify your email and authenticate your domain. If you authenticate your domain, then any email sent from that domain will be less likely to go to spam. For example, if your email is adam@companyx.com, and you verified that email and authenticated, then any other email you send from that domain (for example, sarah@companyx.com) will also be whitelisted from the email client (as long as it's from the same domain name).
3. **Reply To:** If someone wants to reply to your email, you can make the address they reply to different than the sender email (if for example, someone different responds to emails on your team or if you're integrating with a CRM - Customer Relationship Management Software).
4. **Second Subject line (preview text):** Next to the subject line is a field known as the preview text, which acts like a second subject line for you to optimize. This field will only be seen before they open the email, but will not be seen once they open the email. If you leave this field blank, it will

automatically populate this field with the first line of your email.
5. **Actual Subject line:** The main area to optimize is your actual subject line. This is the main thing that a user sees before they open the email. There are a few things to keep in mind when optimizing your subject line:

1. **Length:** The optimal length of an email subject line is about 7 words or 45 characters. It is recommended that you stay in that range since that's the range where you won't have your subject line be cut off in most email clients.
2. **Avoid Spam Words & Phrases:** You need to avoid words or phrases that will trigger the spam filter. Words and phrases like "$$$", "Don't delete", "Free", "Click here" and "I love you", are all examples of this. My general rule is avoid words and phrases that sound "spammy" to you. I also include in the appendix a list of resources to test out for these spam words and phrases.
3. **Make Them Curious:** So, what do you write in the subject line? I recommend thinking of a way to convey what the email is about, but also leave some curiosity as to what the email contains. For example, if I'm writing an email with a special offer for my eCommerce website where users get 30% off on Black Friday, I wouldn't say "Get 30% off this Black Friday on all items", since that gives away all of the information in the subject line, and people would feel like they understood the message and they don't need to open the email. Instead, I would think of a way to say that that would also make people curious of what the email contains. So instead, I might say "A special offer for you this Black Friday", since that would leave people a little more curious on what that special offer is. You may have a different opinion on this, that's why we have to let the data talk, and that leads me to the next point.

4. **A / B Test and Experimentation**: With A/B testing you want to create at least 2 variations of a subject line and see which one does best. How this works is you put in 2 different subject lines into your email client, it will send both to a sample of your audience (which would be the test subjects), then based on the results from that test, it would choose a winner and roll that subject line out to the rest of the emails on your list. You don't even have to use a fancy A/B testing solution to try this. It could be as simple as keeping track of the different subject lines you use in a spreadsheet and look for patterns in the types of subject lines you write, and what resonates most with your users.

Lead Magnets

In terms of impact on your business, the most valuable thing you can get from someone online (besides them paying you money) is to get their email! The problem is, people have become weary to giving out their email to every business. That's why you need to incentivize them to enter their email. By them giving you something valuable (their email), you should also give them something valuable in return, in the form of a **lead magnet**.

From a psychological point of view, having a lead magnet builds reciprocity in your clients by showing them value upfront, which builds your credibility and trust. A lead magnet is something of value that you offer to a user in exchange for getting their details (mainly their email) as a lead. The magnet part of the phrase is meant to signify that you want to attract them like a magnet to enter their details by offering them something of value. Examples of what you can offer your users in a lead magnet are:

A discount or special offer for your product / serviceA free guide (eBook, whitepaper etc.)A free course / webinarA free consultation / call A free trial or demo

When thinking about a lead magnet, I recommend focusing on incentives that are both relevant for your business, and that qualify your leads. For example, you know that if someone is interested in a guide or a free trial, they would potentially be great customers.

Drip Campaigns & Email Automation

When most people think about email, they typically think about sending out newsletters or eShots, which are basically just standard newsletters. However, where email becomes very powerful is when you start to incorporate email automation and drip campaigns.

Email Automation

What makes email an efficient and scalable way of growing your efforts is to incorporate automation into your email marketing strategy. What this means is that you want to send people emails in an automatic way to keep them engaged, and ideally to keep them as long term customers. Next I'll be discussing the methodology of email marketing (you can also view my recommended email tools in the appendix).

Workflow

When defining an email automation strategy, the first thing you need to map out is your **workflow**, this can also be called the email sequence or email series. Put in simple terms, this just defining what are the emails that you automatically want to send out, along with what causes each email to be sent (known as the trigger).

Triggers

The first thing you need to understand about email automation, is that it is based on **triggers**. A trigger is something that you need to define that determines what causes an automation email to be sent. There are 4 main types of triggers.

1) Time based: The first type of trigger is one that is based on time, where you sent an automation email based on time elapsing since an activity is done. For example, you can setup a time-based automation email to be sent to a user 24 hours after they join your list.

2) Email Interaction based: Another way you can trigger an automation email is based on interaction with a previous email sent. For example, you can send a second email if a user opens, clicks or replies to a previous email.

3) Website / App interaction based: You can also send out emails based on something a user done on your website or app, as long as they are logged into the website (so you know what their email is). For example, if a user adds a product to their shopping cart online but doesn't complete their purchase, you can automatically send them an email.

4) Data based: The final way is data or segmentation based. This is where you send a user an email depending on criteria you define from data you already gathered about them. For example, if you store a user's birthday, you can automatically send them a happy birthday email.

Drip Campaigns

Now that you have a basic understanding of email automation, what is a **drip campaign**? A drip campaign is an email automation strategy where you send the user information over time (you drip it out to them) instead of sending them all of the information you want to convey right away by using some of the triggers mentioned above to create a workflow based on the goal of your campaign. Examples of this are:

Lead Validation

If you have a large number of emails (leads) that you want to validate (to see how many of them are relevant to you), you can design a drip campaign around them. For example, let's say you gathered 100 business cards at a conference for potential clients, and you want to know which of the people whose cards you gathered might be interested in becoming a customer of yours. You can send all of them an email, then depending on how they interact with that first email, have automatic follow ups. So, if they open the first email, then you can send them a follow up to schedule a call. If they don't open the first email, you can wait for 3 days, then try sending them another email with a different subject line. If they don't open that email, then you can take them off of your list.

Lead Nurturing

Another popular drip campaign technique is to build a lead nurturing strategy, which has the goal of pushing people down your sales funnel. For example, if someone fills out a lead magnet on your website which would send them free information about your product, you can then automatically trigger an email to go out to have them perform the next action you're planning. That could be them signing up for a free trial or booking a call for example. Then if they perform that action, you can have an automated email go out to push them to the action after that which might be a purchase or sale. The trick with this strategy is you need to map out what you want them to do at each stage, and also follow up with ones that get stuck on a stage (for example if someone stays on step 1 but never progresses to the next level).

Transactional

Besides drip campaigns, another popular way that automated email is used is through **transactional emails**. Transactional emails are usually related to eCommerce websites or transactions as the name suggests. Below are some examples of transactional emails.

Abandoned Cart

This is where you send a user an email reminding them to complete their purchase if they added a product to their shopping cart but did not checkout. The limitation of this method is a user has to be logged into your website, in order for you to send them an email, since otherwise you wouldn't know what their email was. If a user is not logged in and you still want to target them, then the other way that you can do this is by running **remarketing** or **retargeting** ads, since that approach does not need you to have them logged in (since it is based on the browser cookie).

Product Recommendations

Another example of transactional emails is sending a user product recommendations based on previous purchase data. For example, if a user buys a laptop, you can automatically send them an email with products that go together with what they bought like bags or accessories. This technique in the marketing world is known as **cross selling**.

Re-engagement

Re-engagement emails are an example that has to do with increasing your customer lifetime value. The way this works is that you segment your email list based on users that did not buy from you for a long time and try to get them to re-engage or make a new purchase. For example, you could send an email to all of your customers that did not buy from you in the last year and send them an email with a special discount code, to get them to come back.

Action Plan

1. SEO, check the technical issues listed in this chapter for your website.
2. SEO, choose the keywords that you want to start targeting for your website, and start adding them to your pages (this needs to be done on each of your top pages).
3. SEO, start looking for link building opportunities with the methods mentioned.
4. Start building content on your website (start a blog if you can), that answers people's questions in your industry.
5. Social Media, come up with your tone of voice and the types of content you'd like to start sharing.
6. Email, sign up for some email service and start collecting emails.
7. Think of a lead magnet you can give away to people in exchange for their email address.

Chapter 7 - Measuring results

We talked a bit about good and bad results, but that might leave you scratching your head. What makes a result good or bad? Can this be standardized and measured? The answer is yes, if you know what to measure.

The Digital Ad Funnel

There are levels at which you can track the success of your digital marketing campaigns. This may look familiar to you, if you've seen the A,I,D,A (Attention, Interest, Decision and Action) sales model.

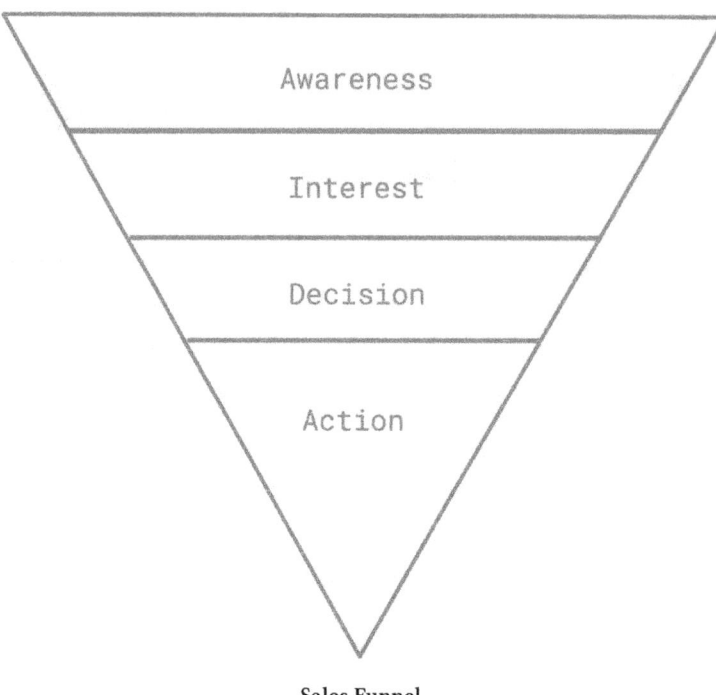

Sales Funnel

As mentioned in chapter 2, in the digital world this can also be summarized as 4 levels in the Digital Ad funnel.

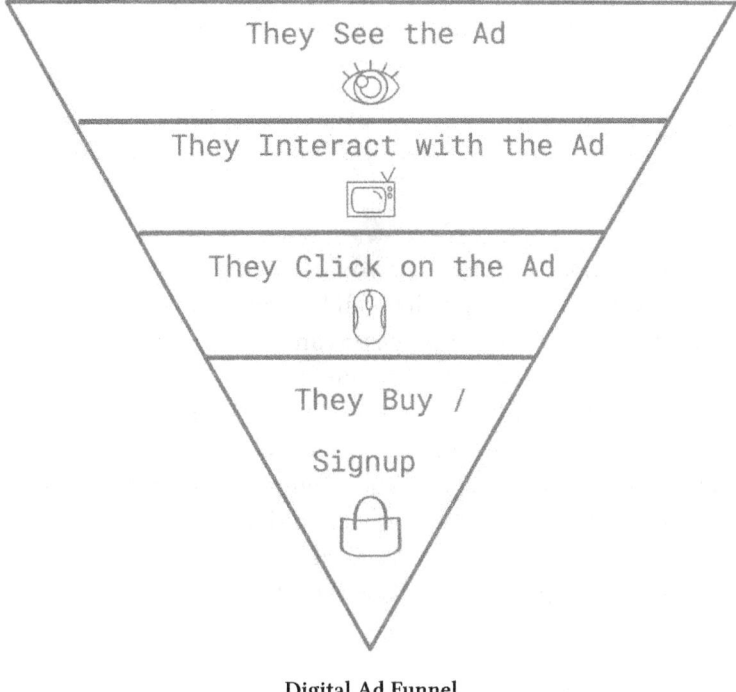

Digital Ad Funnel

For the focus of this chapter, we're going to be spending our time on the lowest level the sale or the conversion in this process. For this, there are 3 things that you should look at, to see if your digital marketing efforts are working.

1 - Conversion Rate

Conversion Rate is calculated by looking at the number of impressions, divided by the number of conversions. This tells you how effective your marketing is.

Your goal is to get that number to be as high as possible.

Let's give an example. Let's say that you bring 100 people onto your website. If one of them does want you want them to do (complete one of your goals by filling up a form for example), then your conversion rate for that goal is 1/100 or 1%.

Per Goal

Each of the different goals on your website / app will have their own conversion rate. For example, if you have 2 goals that you want to track on your site like a purchase and a lead, then you would have 2 conversion rates, one for purchases and one for leads. You would also have an overall conversion rate for both of them together as well, but if you want to optimize them, you would need to look at them separately. Let's say that in this example, you have 1,000 people visit your website, 5 of whom purchase a product and 100 of them signup to learn more (as leads). In that case you would have a conversion rate of 5/1000= 0.5% for purchases, and 100/1000= 10% for leads, and an overall conversion rate of 100+5/1000= 10.5% when you look at conversions and leads together.

Per Channel

In addition to tracking your goals based on how you define them, you also need to split them by their channels (or if you want to be even more specific, by the Source / Medium). So you should know, what is your Conversion Rate for Facebook Paid Ads, what is your Conversion Rate for SEO, and this should be known to you both as an overall basis (by looking at the overall number for all channels), and by looking at each channel on their own.

Per Campaign

When it comes to campaigns you're running (paid campaigns, email campaigns etc) you may also want to track them on an individual basis to see what's working. So, for example, if you were to run 3 marketing campaigns on Facebook ads, you should be able to tell them conversion rate for each of them, to figure out which targeting method worked best.

2- CPA (Cost per acquisition)

Once you have your conversion rate tracked, the next thing you want to start tracking is your CPA or cost per acquisition. I would define CPA as the cost needed to get one person to complete a goal (usually a purchase). So, let's say that you spent $100 on marketing, and you get 10 customers from that spend. In that case, your CPA would be $100/10= $10. What that means is that it on average costs you $10 to acquire a customer through that channel. Of course, you would need to split this in the same way mentioned above (per goal, per channel and per campaign) to see what is working.

What is a good CPA?

In the previous example, we said that the CPA (the cost to get one sale) was $10. Is that a good or bad? Like all things in life, it depends. Let me give you 2 examples of how you can tell if the $10 amount is a good or a bad CPA number. It mainly has to do with the margins of the product or service that you're selling.

CPL

If you are a business that works with leads instead of just looking at CPA, you would also need to look at your CPL (cost per lead). This would have the same methodology of CPA, but instead of your final goal being tied to revenue, you instead tie it to a goal, some of which convert into sales later on (so you need an additional stage that calculates the conversion rate from lead to sale), as mentioned in chapter 3.

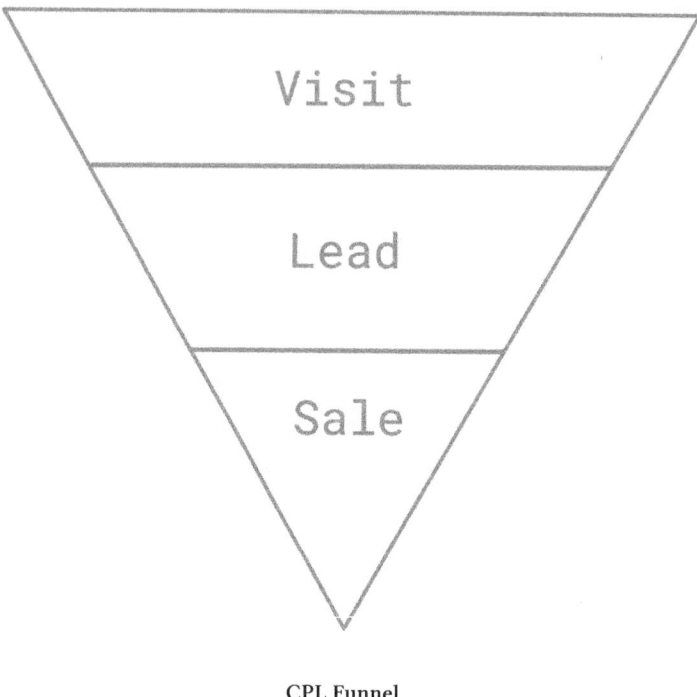

CPL Funnel

3- Revenue, Margins and Profit

As a business, you're selling something. At some point in the organization you want to charge people for something (otherwise it's not a business, but a non-profit). The goal of your marketing should essentially be to get more sales and more customers. To be effective in marketing, what you need to do is look at how much revenue you make per order. That is known as your **Revenue**.

A top level way of doing this is measuring your Return on Ad Spend

(**ROAS**), which is basically just a measure of how much revenue did you make from your marketing costs (for example, if you spend $10 and make $100 in revenue, your ROAS is 100/10, which comes to 10:1 or 1000%)

After that, what you then need to look at is your **Profit**, which you calculate by taking your Revenue and subtracting all of the costs associated with that sale from it.

This is not a book on how to build a business, but some common costs you'll have in your business are:

- Marketing
- Logistics & Delivery Costs
- Salaries
- Administrative Expenses
- Licensing Expenses
- A lot more I haven't mentioned here

So basically, in order to be a profitable business, you have to take all of your Revenue and subtract all of your costs (marketing being one of those costs).

So, the question is, how much is a good amount to spend on marketing for your business?

The ideal answer is zero. In a perfect world, you would want to spend zero on your marketing, but unfortunately that's not possible as business is competitive. So, what is a good amount?

That's why looking at CPA is very important, with regards to your budget and marketing spend, because it lets you know if you have a good ROI (return on investment) for what you're spending.

My general rule of thumb is that for a healthy business, your marketing spend should ideally be less than 20% of your Revenue generated. This might be higher or lower depending on the business, but it's a good rule of thumb to follow if you're not sure where to start.

Let's take a couple of examples, where we look at how you

1. Selling Clothing (eCommerce store)

Your Average Revenue per item sold: $50 Other Estimated Costs (shipping, delivery, hosting costs etc.) per item sold: $10

It the above scenario, what do you think a good number to spend on marketing is? Again, the ideal scenario is to spend zero, so you make a profit of $50-$10= $40 per item profit. However, you're probably not constantly selling every item you have, you need to market it. So what number is good to start? Of course, this depends on your business, and you can try any numbers that make sense, but my recommendation in the above case is not to spend more than 20% of $50, i.e. a $10 CPA. So therefore, if you sell one item, you'll make a profit of 50-10-10= $30.

It is possible to spend more on marketing, and still make a profit? Probably, but what I'm suggesting is the ideal scenario to start with as a rule of thumb.

2. Selling Real Estate Your Average Revenue per item sold (your commission): $7,000 Other estimated costs (agency fees, insurance, government fees): $1,000

Now in the above scenario, for every item you sell, you make $7,000-$1,000= $6,000 when you don't account for marketing. So that means that you have a lot more area to play with for your profitability. Of course, you want to make as much money as possible, but it means that you can afford if you need to, to spend more for your CPA. In the above case, if I take a 20% number based on my total revenue then that means that I can spend up to $1,400 as a CPA to get one sale. That is a lot higher than our first example, but it is still profitable. Keep in mind though that there may be an extra step that you need to worry about before you get someone to buy from you in this example.

Working Backwards to CPA

What are the typical steps that someone goes through whenever they make a purchase? That depends on the type of product or service you're selling. Usually there are the following steps, this is known as the "Digital Sales Funnel" (mentioned earlier).

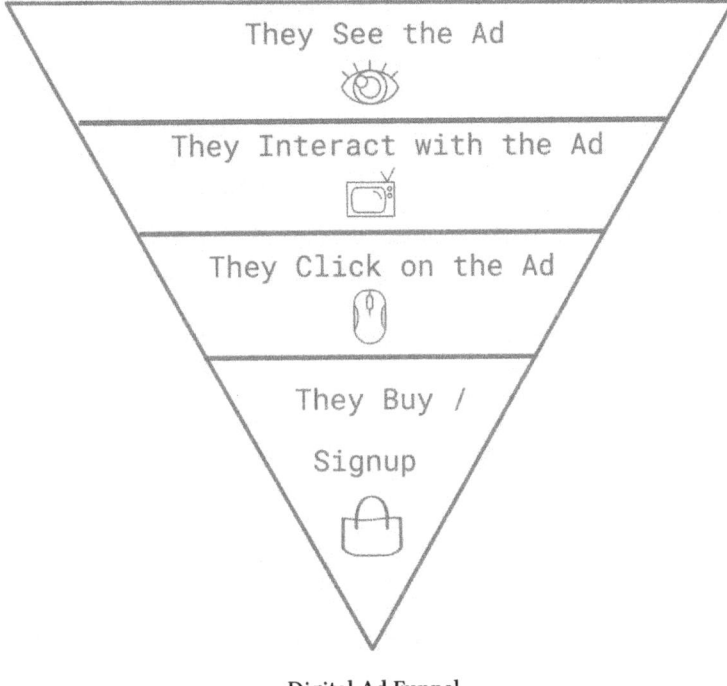

Digital Ad Funnel

Let's say that you define your target CPA to be $10. In order to see what to spend for your marketing, you just have to work backwards to estimate what your CPC and then CPM is for that CPA amount, by looking at your estimated Conversion Rate and Click Through Rate (CTR).

If you need a $10 CPA, and your Conversion rate is 1%, that means that you need to get 100 clicks to get one conversion. That also means you can estimate your CPC to be 10/100 or $0.1.

For your CPM, if your CTR (click through rate) is 2%, that means that you need 100 impressions to get 2 clicks. To calculate your CPM (the amount it costs for 1,000 impressions), that means that you need to get 500 impressions for every 100 clicks. Therefore, your CPM rate would have to be $20 for every one sale (since for every 1000 impressions, you would get 200 clicks, which would get you 2 sales for a CPA of $10).

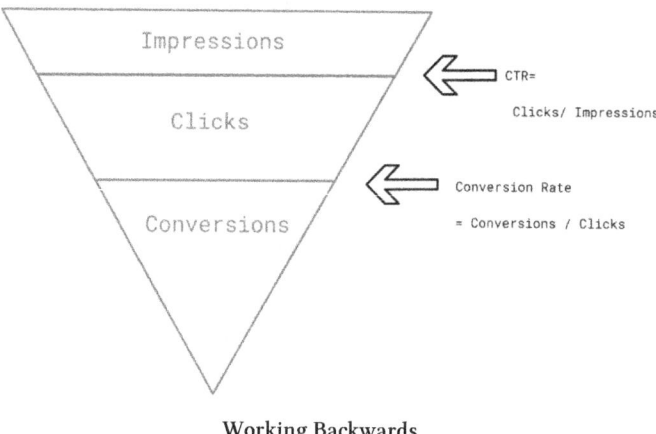

Working Backwards

CPL Instead of CPA

You may have another step between clicks and purchases, however, known as leads. This is often the case if you are selling a B2B service (e.g. consulting services) or if you have a product that has a high-ticket price.

That would make your digital sales funnel look like this:

· Impressions

· Clicks

· Leads

· Conversions

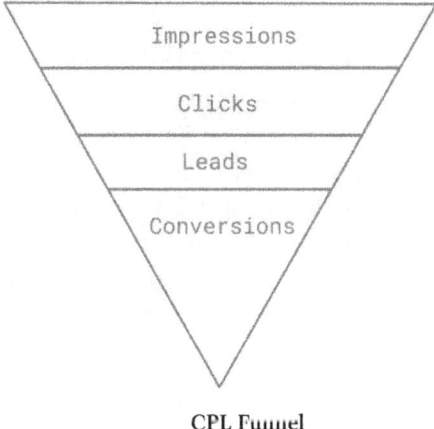

CPL Funnel

In that case, leads are either

1. Fed into a CRM (Customer Relationship Management) tool, with someone following up to close the deal (a salesperson),

or

2. Automatically followed up with using automated email campaigns (drip campaigns).

From a practical point of view, this doesn't make much of a difference, just that there is an extra step needed (to follow up on a lead in some way), before they make a purchase.

Setting a Budget

One of the most common questions people have when starting to market a business, is "what do I set my budget to?" If you are working for a company in their marketing department, it's very likely that you already have a marketing budget with KPI's (key performance indicators, i.e. targets), but what if that's not the case? You might be running marketing for your own business or the one who had to set the marketing budget in a larger company. So how do you start?

It's the same way I mentioned earlier, by looking at the CPA (cost per acquisition) relative to your profitability just expanded to the number of orders you want to achieve. For example, if you're selling an item whose revenue per item is $100, and you set your marketing to a $20 CPA for profitability, you just have to estimate the number of orders you want to reach. Let's say that you want 100 orders (or a revenue of $100*100=$10,000), in that case it means that you would need to spend $20*100= $2,000. So that means that your marketing budget is $2,000 for the month.

It's important though, that you keep in mind that your $2,000 a month budget, does not guarantee that you will get 100 orders. This is just an estimate, because there are 2 main constraints that might limit if this goal can be achieved, so they both need to be accounted for.

Your conversion Rate

The main factor that would constrain you reaching your goal, is your conversion rate. Again, the conversion rate is the number of goals you achieve, relative to the number of clicks or visits you receive. So, for example, if you get 2 conversions for every 100 visits that visit your site, then your conversion rate is 2%.

Extrapolating this out to the example we gave earlier with our

$2,000 a month budget, that means that we should get at least 100 orders from that amount (based on the CPA we mentioned earlier), and for our conversion rate, if we assume the same value of 2%, that means that we have to get 5,000 visits or clicks, since 100 (the number of orders) is 2% (our expected conversion rate of 5,000 (the number of visits we need).

Bidding CPA

If we wanted to bid CPA, it's simple. We just need to make our CPA bid be the amount we estimated earlier, which is $20. That just means that you're not willing to spend more than $20 on marketing per sale or purchase you get.

Bidding CPC

If we were bidding CPC, if we want to calculate our maximum CPC, we just plug in the formula: Maximum CPC = Monthly Budget / Expected Needed Visits (based on conversion rate).

That would mean that we cannot spend more than 2000/5000 = $0.4 per click, so our average CPC cannot exceed $0.4.

Bidding CPM

If we were bidding CPM, we would just have to go back one more layer (to the impression level), calculate our CTR (Click Through Rate), and then work down until we get to our CPC and then CPA number.

For example, if we know that our CTR is 2% on average, that means that for every 1000 impressions we get (our CPM), only 2% of 1000, or 20 of them will actually click on the ad. In this example, let's say that our CPM rate is $20. That means that for every $20, that would buy you 1000 impressions, which (according to our CTR number), would mean we would get 20 clicks. So, in essence, we're paying

$20 for 20 clicks (or a $1 CPC). Of course, we can improve this by having a better CTR, which can be accomplished by having better ads and better targeting, and that in turn would give us a better CPC number.

Budget plateauing

Throughout this exercise, you might be thinking to yourself, "Why even set a budget limit?" As long as ROI (return on investment) is positive, and you're getting the CPA that you want, then why even limit the budget? Won't the company just keep growing if you keep spending more within the budget that you set? This way of thinking may seem to make logical sense (oftentimes it does), however, a key factor that you need to consider when making budgeting decisions for your business is the fact that budgets plateau.

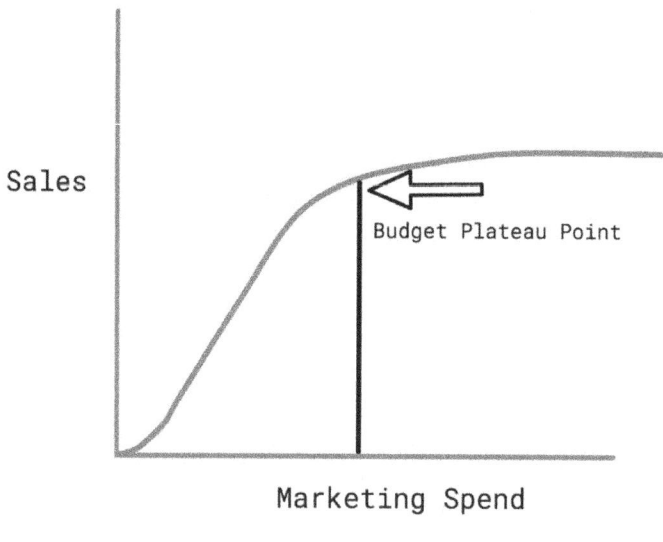

Budget Plateau

Eventually, you will reach a stage of diminishing returns, and it will reach a point that the more money you spend, the higher your CPA will be, but the numbers of orders or sign ups won't go up. The reason this is the case is because in the end of the day, the size of the pool of people that you are targeting is limited. For example, if there are 1,000 people you are targeting that would all buy your product, you may reach them all for $100 (you're maxing out your audience), in which case it wouldn't make a difference if you spent $100, $1000 or even $1,000,000, because the size of the audience wouldn't change. Therefore, spending more would only make your CPA go up, since there is no one left to buy in your audience (it would either keep showing the same ads to the same people, or show your ad to people that are not interested in what you offer).

Reaching your optimal level

So how do you reach the optimal level? Ideally you want to be at the stage where you are making the most amount of revenue, while at the same time, you're within the CPA limit that you set for yourself. This requires testing different bids, budgets and targeting methods to find that sweet spot. Keep in mind though, that is could be a moving target as overnight your audience might change, other competitors might enter the market, or you might make improvements to your product (or pricing), that your audience finds appealing, which would have an effect on your CPA and in turn what plateau level you reach.

CAC (Cost per Acquisition of Customer) and ***CLV (Customer Lifetime Value).***

There are some cases in which you would actually not care about immediate profitability. These are business where you are more customer focused than transaction focused.

The main types of businesses that would fall under this model are any business that has recurring customers, recurring fees or subscription fees.

(We'll go over this in more detail in Chapter 10)

Now where the real value of this lies is when you look at something known as the *Customer Lifetime Value*. The customer lifetime value is a measure of how much monetary value a customer brings you in their lifetime (or how long they stay a customer for). For example, if we take the example of someone subscribing to a service at $15 a month, and they on average stay as a customer for 2 years, we can calculate the Customer Lifetime Value (CLV) by multiplying the amount of revenue that they generate over their total period as a customer, which in this example would be $15 x 24 (number of months in 2 years) = $360.

How does this change how we think about marketing? Mainly it goes back to the discussion of CPA as a percentage of your revenue. Since now we're looking at the CLV, we take a customer rather than a transaction look at how we acquire customer, so we look at the CAC number. In this scenario, we can spend a lot more on marketing, because we can project that we'll eventually get all of that money back.

This can get a little messy, since often times when a company is growing at a rapid rate, they may see that it's better to hold off on profitability. So even if your company does lend itself to the CLV model, there are a couple of levels of growth that you can choose from:

Level 1: Be profitable on CAC

This is where you make sure that you are profitable from the first transaction (the CAC number), which in actuality is the same as optimizing for CPA. This is the example I gave earlier, where is the price of your subscription is $15 a month, you target a CPA of 20% of that, which would be $3. This is the safe option, but would make it harder for you to grow since your marketing budget would be reduced (and your competitors might not have the same constraint).

Level 2: Be profitable on perceived CLV

The more aggressive way of budgeting is to take a percentage based on the perceived Customer Lifetime Value (CLV). If we take the above example and say that our subscription is $15 and the expected CLV is $360, then that means that we target to have a CPA value of $72 (if we target a 20% CPA number).

So, you can see the difference. If we target the first option, we can only spend $3 per signup, but if we target the second option, we can have a marketing budget of $72 per signup, which is a 24 times higher CPA value! Given those two options, which company do you think would grow faster? Of course, the second one. This runs the risk of you not making back the amount, however, if your customer lifetime estimates are off. That's why this approach is usually only taken when either: a) You have a lot of historical data and can estimate what your perceived customer lifetime value will be or b) You want to grow very quickly and cash flow is not that important for you. This is the approach of companies that are VC (venture capital) funded that want to grow at all costs. Of course, this way is very risky since you're basically spending money you don't have for a perceived gain, but then again that's why so many VC startups fail.

Whichever of the methods best suits your business, my initial recommendation is always to estimate your budget first and keep iterating until you reach your ideal profitability number.

Multichannel Attribution

A very important concept you need to understand as a marketing person is that the average user usually needs to visit your site or app multiple times before they take action. It depends on the service or product, but from what I've seen most users need to visit a website on average 3 times before they make an initial purchase. The problem this causes for marketers, is that most reporting only looks at the final channel a user comes from before they made a purchase, while ignoring the others.

For example, let's say that a user finds out about you from a YouTube ad, and visits your site, but doesn't buy anything. Then the next day, that same user, does a Google search about your product, visits your website, but still doesn't buy. Now let's say on the third day, that same user, looks for you on Instagram, goes to your profile there, clicks on the link in your profile to go to your website, and then makes a purchase.

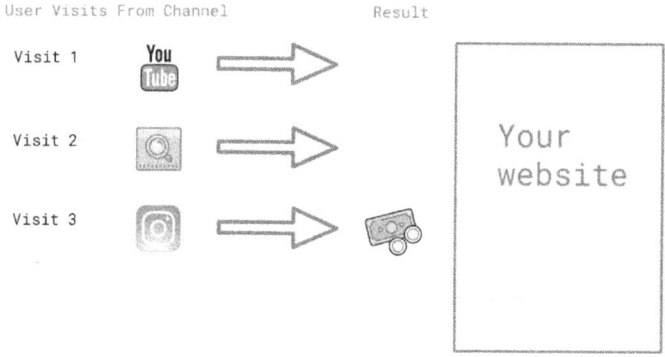

Multi Channel Attribution

In that example, you would open your analytics dashboard and see you have 1 sale from Instagram, but does that paint the whole picture? Not really, because in that case you might think that your YouTube ads are worthless, so you would stop spending on them, which in the future would affect your revenue.

Attribution Models

The way of tracking highlighted above is known as "Last Click" attribution, since you are giving 100% of the credit to the last channel that brought that customer while ignoring the rest.

Channel Teamwork

An illustrative way to think about how a user completes an action on your site is a bit like a football team. When someone scores a goal, when you look at the last click it's like you're giving 100% of the credit for the team winning to the striker that scored the goal, and 0% to the goalie, defenders, and midfielders. You can see how this can be misleading, since if you suddenly took out all of the players on the team, except for the offensive striker, there is no way the team would still win.

So, what is the right way to look at your website conversions? Well, there is no 100% right answer, but there are a few different models that you should consider whenever you're making a decision on where to focus your efforts.

Last click: This is the example we just mentioned. In last click attribution, 100% of the conversion is given to the last channel a user came from, before they completed the action.

Time Decay: With time decay, more credit is given the closer a user is to the last channel. For example, if a user visited your site through 4 channels, 10% might be attributed to the first channel, 20% to the second, 30% to the third and 40% to the last channel.

Linear: This model gives an equal percentage to every single channel. For example, if a user visited your site from 10 different channels before they made a purchase, it will give 10% to each stage of the funnel. While this seems fair, the disadvantage of this model is that from a user point of view, usually the first and last channels are the most impactful when it comes to behavior.

Position Based: With position-based attribution, most credit is given to the first and last channel, while the rest is distributed to the middle channels. For example, if a user visited your site through

10 different channels, 40% might be attributed to both the first and last channel, while the remaining 20% would be distributed to the remaining 8 middle channels.

First Click: First click is when you give 100% of the credit to the first channel a user visited your website through, and 0% to all of the subsequent channels (including the last channel). First click is useful to see where users initially hear about your product or brand and is used mainly when companies are looking to expose their products to new customers and markets.

Platform Specific: The large ad platforms (like Google and Facebook), also provide their own attribution models that combine a number of factors with their own data, along with data they gather from your own platform. I recommend testing them out, since they are very useful when it comes to optimizing your ad spend, as they can help you get a better Return on Investment (ROI).

There is no right way of tracking attribution, as all of the above ways show a different side of the story. In practical terms, most marketing efforts are still done on a last click basis. However, it is important to keep in mind that at the very least, you should regularly look into the full journey of your customers and look into your multi-channel reporting to see if you notice any trends that you can use in your marketing strategy.

Action Plan

1. Start tracking your Conversion rate on an overall, per goal and per channel basis
2. Start tracking your CPA on an overall, per goal and per channel basis
3. Track your initial ROAS for overall Revenue and Cost
4. Make sure to track your marketing budget against your margins and profits including your multi-channel attribution

5. Define your initial marketing budget (starting on a monthly basis)

Chapter 8 - What do you do if it's working?

Now that you know how to launch a campaign, plan a budget, and measure results, two things might happen. It would either work or it wouldn't.

Let's take the best-case scenario and assume that it worked. How can we tell it worked? To recap, based on what was mentioned in the previous section, we would see if our marketing spend is in line with our profitability, as a percentage of our total revenue to make sure that our marketing spend is profitable.

If we do notice that it's working, our work is not done. As a marketing person you need to be able to constantly optimize and improve your campaign performance, because stability is not something that is guaranteed in digital marketing. This means a few things.

Bringing down our CPA

If you have a revenue per product of $100, and your marketing spend is $20, that's great, you seem to be doing well. You're making $5 for every $1 that you spend on marketing. What happens next though, is you (or your manager) are not satisfied. Why not try for $6 for every $1, or $10 or $100 for every $1 of marketing spend. This may seem unrealistic, but you never know until you try it. Just because something is working, it doesn't mean you should get comfortable. You have to find the optimal point or "goldilocks zone" for your marketing efforts, and even if things are working now, they could be even better.

Playing with your levers to find the optimal level

So how can you go about testing to find the optimal level? It boils down to 5 things that you can play with:

1. Your bid (how much you're paying on a per impression, per click, or per acquisition basis)
2. Your budget
3. Your creatives, or the ads that you run. This entails trying different videos, images, and messaging on your ad, until you find one that resonates.
4. Your targeting methods, or the audience you're targeting. It might be that your assumption of your audience is wrong. If that's the case, then trying a different audience (even a slight tweak like slightly changing the age range or location targeting) could make a big difference.
5. The landing page or product that you're targeting. In this case, it can refer to either the landing page (the section of your site) where they wind up, what messaging is on the site, or the product itself. This is the last stage of the funnel and can often times have the biggest wins for the smallest effort.

Each of these areas can be optimized at different stages of the funnel.

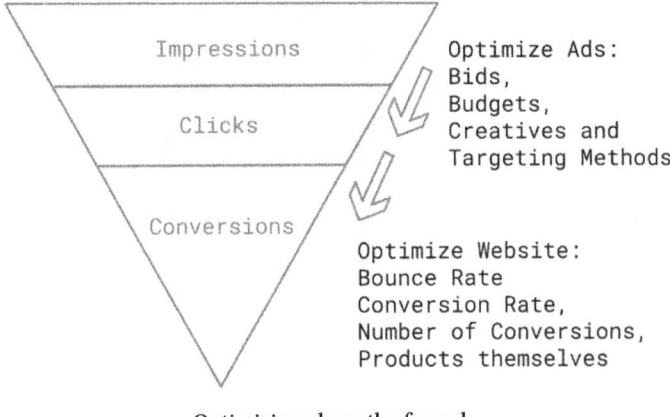

Optimizing along the funnel

Breaking this down like this, allows you to make changes at every level, which leads to overall better results.

Beware of the budget plateau

Although I mentioned this earlier, it's worth reiterating in this section. Whenever you're spending on marketing, if you get positive results you may think that by just scaling up how much you spend, you'll get similar results. For example, if you're spending $1,000 and getting a marketing return CPA of $10 with 100 orders, then you might think, why not spend $2,000 and get 200 orders! You need to be careful with this line of thinking though, because of a concept known as the budget plateau. Whenever you're spending on a certain targeting method with a certain audience, eventually you will reach a plateau, because the size of your audience is limited, and no matter how much money you pour at something, it can't change the fact that you can't force the size of the audience to grow.

Another way that you could reach this plateau stage is if your ads get stale. You need to constantly refresh your ads to avoid **ad blindness** (the fact that if your audience keeps seeing the same ad from you over a long period of time, they'll automatically start ignoring it because they'll think they already know what you'll say).

There also may be a point when you reach diminishing returns. If you exhausted your audience, it's quite possible that besides even plateauing, your sales might actually go down, despite higher marketing spend.

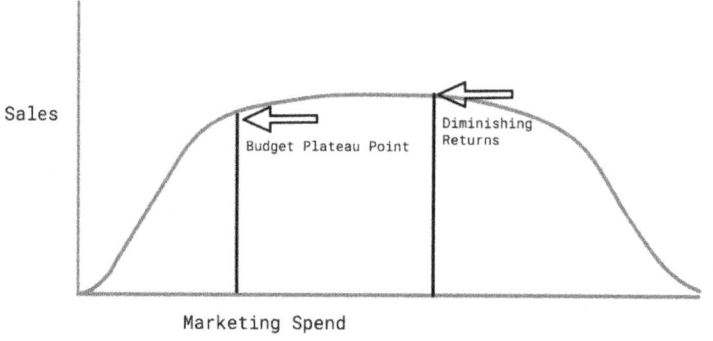

Budget Plateau Level

So, what do you do if you want to scale up and avoid this problem?

The main trick is that once you have a marketing campaign that's working, you want to test different budgets and bids to find the sweet spot. That means changing your bids (which could be CPM, CPV, CPC, or CPA), as well as your daily budgets, until you find the optimal sweet spot, where you get either: a) The best CPA b) The most orders (sales) c) The most profit

These 3 levers are ones that may be prioritized differently depending on the current goal you have.

Let me give a few examples of this.

CPA	Cost	Orders	Revenue	Profit
$35	$3,500	100	$6,000	$2,500
$10	$500	50	$2,500	$2,000
$15	$900	60	$3,600	$2,700

Optimal Level Example

So, which of these is the best? That depends on what you're prioritizing. If you don't have a large budget and you don't feel comfortable spending a lot (because of cash flow issues etc.), then you may want to prioritize the low-cost option low CPA option. If your priority is growth in the short term, then you might just care about the total number of orders, while profitability would be less important. If you want to be as profitable as possible, and initial cost is less of an issue, you would choose the option that gives you the profitability and so on. It all depends on your priorities as a business.

Action Plan

1. Optimize your campaigns as the 3 levels of the ad funnel
2. Once you launch your campaigns, choose your optimization strategy (best CPA, more sales or more leads)
3. Learn to reach your optimal spend level and avoid budget plateauing by frequently changing your ads (at least once a month) and optimizing your bids and budgets.

Chapter 9 - What to do if it's not working?

One of the most frustrating things about digital marketing is when you think you did everything right, but things are just not working. You follow this book, or another strategy you were told would work, but you're not getting the results you want. You feel frustrated and don't know what path to take. You may even be thinking that digital marketing is not for you, and you should try another approach to grow your business. I know it can be very annoying when things aren't working and you feel like you're wasting money, but don't worry, that's what I'm here to help you with.

Before I start giving you solutions on how to figure out why things didn't work, let's first look into what we mean by "things didn't work." The first step is to diagnose the problem and see if there are ways to remedy our marketing before calling it quits.

Let's go over the areas that could go wrong. Usually whenever someone says marketing is not working, it's usually for one of two reasons. Either:

1. **Spending too much without results**: This has to do with the return on investment (ROI) of your efforts. This could be on a revenue versus cost level or a revenue versus profit level. This is the most obvious case of marketing not working, you're just spending too much money and not getting enough return on that spend.
2. **Not growing fast enough**: The other way that your marketing could be not working, is you're simply not growing fast enough. You're trying various techniques and none of them

are getting any traction, or you are getting some traction but not enough where it makes sense for the business.

Once you diagnose what exactly is not working in your marketing efforts, you can begin to take measures to start moving things in the right direction. I recommend looking at the following categories for areas of improvement:

Change the targeting

The first thing that should look into if something is not working in your marketing is your targeting. Your targeting is the starting point of where your ad shows up, so when something is not working it's the first place to start. So, how can you change your targeting when something is not working? There are a few areas you can look into:

• Different Audience Targeting: It could be that the audience you chose is not the right one and that the initial assumption you had was wrong. Are you targeting women, when you should be targeting men? Are you targeting people in the city, when you should be targeting people in the suburbs? You may need to retest the assumptions you initially had about your audience.

• Different ways to reach that audience: Let's say that you are confident you are targeting the right audience. The next area you need to optimize for is how do you reach that audience. Is your audience single moms who love to cycle? It's great that you know your audience, but it could be that you're not reaching them properly. Some channels (like Facebook / Instagram), let you target your customers directly based on demographics data. Other channels like Google Search can let you target users based on what they're searching for. However, other channels (like Google Display), need you instead to target the behavior of the user online. This can be showing your ads on websites that your users frequent. Do your customers also frequently browse finance websites, or blogs that talk about motherhood? That's something that you need to find out about your customers by testing out different targeting methods to test your assumptions. It could just be a matter of finding where they congregate. This can also be referred to as "water holing" or looking for where they hang out in groups: what websites, blogs, vlogs, apps do they frequent.

- Playing with the audience size: Another tactic you might want to employ is to expand your audience. If you target a niche that is too small, even if they are your ideal customers, there just might not be enough of them. On the flip side though, you don't want your audience to be too wide either, since a large audience might show your ad outside of your target audience. So, what should you do? How do you find the sweet spot of audience size? To start, each of the ad platforms online (Facebook / Instagram, Twitter, LinkedIn, Snapchat etc.), all have a built-in optimal audience size graph.

Audience Definition

Specific   Broad

Your audience is defined.

Potential Reach: 320,000 people

Audience Size

Of course, this can be biased, as often times the ad platforms just want you to spend more money on their platform, so they'll say that you need a large audience size.

Reach versus Paid Impressions

A common distinction you should know about is the difference between **reach** and **paid impressions**. Your reach is how many people you could potentially show your ad to *if* your bids and budgets were unlimited. For example, if I create an ad on Google and it tells me based on my targeting method it could reach 100,000 people, that number is based on if I have no cap on my bids and budgets.

However, once I plug in what I'm willing to pay (my CPM, CPV, CPC or CPA and my budget), I'll get another value known as my **paid impressions** which is how much I'm expected to realistically reach based on the monetary constraints I set.

Reach versus Impressions

Based on my experience, the size of your audience depends on your business, and your budget. As a general rule of thumb though, I would say that for every $100 that you spend, your paid impressions audience should be at least 5,000 people (if we assume an industry average CPM rate of $2).

If you start with a minimum audience size, it could be that you maxed it out. So, you may need to expand the audience by a factor of at least 2, in order to run another test.

Audience size and conversion optimization

The only time when I would say that the audience doesn't matter as much, is in the case of when you're running campaigns that are optimized for conversions (CPA based targeting), since in that case even if you have a large audience (of a million or more people), the ad platform will automatically target individually it deems more likely to convert within your audience (based on the many touch points it looks at in its own system). So for example, if you're running a CPA campaign on Facebook and your audience size is one million people based on the targeting you chose (this is known as your **audience reach**), it may only show the ad to 10,000 people, since based on the data the platform gathered from your historical conversions, the bid you set and your budget, that's the size of my ideal customer base.

Change the ads

The next area you would look into changing are the ads. In digital terms, these are also known as the "creatives", which are either the images or videos that you use in your ads. If your CTR (click through rate), or engagement rate is low, then changing the ads could improve them. You can improve them by changing the design, coming up with better images and videos (now all major ad platforms have built in image and video creation tools, or you could use an online service, like Canva and stock pictures from Unsplash), testing out different CTA's (calls to action, which are active verbs like "Book", "Shop", "Discover", "Learn more"), or testing out different USP's (unique selling points, like prices, promotions or special features in your product or service).

A/B testing

An automated way that this testing could be done is through A/B testing. A/B means testing 2 variations of something for a period of time (testing one variation), then seeing which one is the winner. For example, if you have 2 ads, one with a red background and one with a blue background, and you are targeting to show your ad to 10,000 people, you could run an A/B test to 1,000 people (showing 500 to the red ad, and 500 the blue ad), see which one has more clicks or a higher CTR (click through rate). Once you have a winner during the test phase, you then roll out the winner over the remaining audience you want to target (in this case, 10,000 minus 1,000 or 9,000 people).

Most ad platforms now (Facebook and Google), have built in A/B testing capabilities, so you can just create multiple ads, turn that feature on, and then the platform will run the test for you, and choose the winner (usually based on CTR, or engagement).

Adjust the bids / budgets

The next thing to adjust if things are not working is the bid or budgets. There are two scenarios that could take place that you need to optimize for.

- a. Not spending enough: This is actually very common. If people are more conservative in their marketing, they may be either not bidding enough, or their budgets might not be high enough for the bids they set, so their campaign is not getting enough bids in the auction. The solution to this is to raise the bids and budgets.
- b. Spending too much: The flip side of not spending enough is spending too much. This would be the case (if we assume there are no issues with your targeting or ads) if you have

reached the budget plateau (as mentioned previously). In this case, the solution is to lower your bids or budget until you reach the peak of your profitability.

Softer conversions

Another place that you might need to optimize is your conversion funnel. People often look at the high-level number of conversion rate, if it's low they'll like well I should try something else. But one area that is often overlooked is to actually try a softer conversion rate. This goes back to the famous marketing funnel A,I,D,A (Attention, Interest, Decision, Action) that we mentioned earlier.

If your product is complicated, expensive or both, then you may need to try a softer way to get them into your funnel.

For example, if you want someone to $1,000 piece of software from you, that is a hard conversion to have completely online because it has a high price point. What you can do instead is have a softer conversion of getting them to test the product, schedule a call, or get some kind of demo into how it works first. That would bring more people into the top of your marketing funnel and would give you another data point to work with, instead of just trying to get people to go for the harder conversion (directly making a purchase) right away.

Change the landing page

Once you market to people and bring them on your page or app, what's next? You need to get them to convert! You can have the most optimized marketing funnel in the world, but if at the end of the day your product or service is not appealing, you won't succeed. The first thing to change this is to optimize your landing page. From my experience, a good landing page has 6 things:

1. **Headline value proposition**: This is the condensed version of what you offer as a headline. It directly addresses the problem you're solving. For example, "We make ordering pet food simple".
2. **A Hero image / video**: This is more of a visual thing, but usually a nice landing page with have either imagery or a nice video that talks about your business. Nowadays this doesn't have to be professionally done, there are countless services where you can get high quality pictures, graphics and videos for very low cost (even free).
3. **A call to action tied to the product / service**: It's important to have a clear next step for the user to take once they're on your page. Think of your landing page like a road: it has to lead somewhere. You have to send them to their next destination, which is your "goal" or "conversion". This conversion should be tied with a call to action. For example, if you want people to sign up for a free trial for your pet sitting service, then you could say "Get started pet sitting for free!" and link the button to the free trial page.
4. **Lead form**: Your call to action has to tie in with the next action. This usually takes the form of a "lead magnet". A lead magnet is something that you give away in exchange for that people signing up as a lead. An added benefit of giving something away, is it creates reciprocity in the person you're giving the info to. If you give someone something (even a small gift) it makes them want to return the favor on some level, which could lead to them being more likely to buy from you. This usually takes the form of a goal / conversion. It's recommended though to make it easy for people to get started with a form (as opposed to trying to get everyone to buy). Emails are valuable. "Besides money, the most valuable thing someone can give you online, is their email!"

Think about what you can give people in exchange for that email. This is known as a "Lead magnet". Examples of this are:

- Free samples
- Discount
- Brochure
- Short eBook
- Video content
- Entry into a draw

Choose the one that works best for your business and get started!

A couple of ways that you can increase your effectiveness for this is:

a. **Have an auto-generated email**: You don't want people to wait to hear back. You can connect to a number of services, that will allow you to send emails as soon as someone fills out the form. Attached to that email you'll send them their lead magnet prize (as a pdf etc.).
b. **Link it to a CRM system**: To make things even more effective, you need to link the email / lead coming in, into some kind of CRM or customer relationship management software. This will allow you to see how many leads are in your pipeline and what is their status.

5. **Benefit Statements**: The next thing you should have on your page are benefit statements. Benefit statements are anything that shows people why they should care about your product/service. This is usually your unique selling points (USP's). I recommend having at least three (could be prices, features, ease of use etc.). I recommend keeping language focused on the value you give to users, and how it helps their lives. For example, helping you save money on lead generation etc.

6. **Social proof**: The final area that is important in a landing page is having social proof. Human beings are social creatures, and often look to the group to see if something makes

sense (if you want detailed case studies on why social proof is important, I recommend you read "Influence" by Robert Cialdini). So how can you have social proof? The main ways are:

a. Testimonials: By having quotes from people on how they liked your product or service, it shows others that they can trust you. Having their picture, full name, and where they work also helps show they are real. Some people even include mentions on social media, linking directly to that person's post, to show that they really said it.
b. Partner Logos: This is one that is generally less effective than using real people, but if you don't have any testimonials yet, it can lend credibility. This could be a group of logos of people that you worked with, tools you work with, or even "as seen on" as places that mentioned you in the news. Some companies are strict about using their logos, but especially if you're a small business, as long as you don't say they specifically endorse you, I haven't found this to be a legal problem (I can't give legal advice though, so talk to a lawyer if in doubt).
c. About us: Another way you can show social proof is instead of focusing on the company, focus on the team, especially if the team is of high caliber and has a good reputation.

Once you add these elements to the landing page, you can go about testing different variations. This can be done through A/B testing tools to see how your conversion rate changes based on variations.

Change the price

The next thing to think about changing on your page is the price. It's possible that your customers are interested in your product, but the listed price is too high. Ways that you can test this are:

a. List the product without a price and see if anything changes. If they click to learn more without a price, then the price could be a barrier.
b. Break the price down by showing value-based pricing as opposed to just an amount. For example, you could mention more details on what a user would get by signing up to your service, they just might need to be convinced it's worth it
c. Try a different price: You might think I would just tell you to lower your prices, but you actually need to try to both raise and lower your price to find the perfect equilibrium. I found that bootstrapped startups (startups that aren't venture funded) tend to not charge enough, while others tend to charge too much. The answer goes back to basics economics: finding the optimal point in the supply / demand curve where you achieve the most profitability.

Change the product

What if you tried all of the marketing strategies I mentioned in this book and still nothing works? You tried a bunch of channels, spend hundreds of dollars and still nothing works. The answer might just be that your product /service is not something that the market wants. This is a hard realization to come by, but at the end of the day no marketing in the world can sell a bad product. Product development is outside of the scope of this book, but you may consider tweaking your product or changing the product completely.

Action Plan

If your marketing is not working, use one of the methods outlined in this chapter, which include changing your:

Targeting, Ads, Bids / Budgets, Softer Conversions, Landing Page, Price or Product.

Chapter 10 - Strategies for Growth

There are many ways to achieve growth. Some people call it growth hacking, but I like to call it consistent timeless digital marketing (not as catchy, I know). In this section, I'm going to talk about how you can achieve growth, by following one of the following tried and tested strategies. You may choose only one, or a combination of multiple tactics, depending on what works for your business. These strategies are sorted from most to least costly.

Strategy 1 Long term CLV

The first strategy you can employ is the long-term customer lifetime value strategy. With this method, you don't focus on immediate profitability of a transaction (a single order), but instead focus on the long-term profitability of a customer (who would make multiple orders). In this method, you care less about how much a customer makes once, but instead focus on how much revenue they generate over their lifetime as a customer. Some businesses are more likely to gravitate towards this model, that include:

- SAAS
- eCommerce (brands)
- Subscription services (Netflix etc.)
- Content or Educational websites

If your business is one where you want to build recurring revenue, or multiple transactions over time, then you should look for the CLV (Customer Lifetime Value) approach.

Calculating CAC

The CAC (cost per acquisition of a new customer), is calculated in the same way that you calculate CPA. It's just the amount of marketing spend needed to acquire one new customer. The only difference between CAC and CPA, is that CAC is a measure that only looks at **new customers**, (people that bought for the first time), while CPA looks at just orders, which could contain new customers and repeat buyers. So essentially, your CAC and CPA will have the same value, the only difference is for CAC you have to check if they are a new customer and filter out if they already bought before.

CLV Case Study

Let's give an example of how this strategy works. Let's say you're running marketing for a subscription service where users pay every month (like Netflix). In that case, you have the luxury of not making your money back right away, since you can calculate the average lifetime of your customers and estimate how long a customer will stay with you. For example, if based on your data you see that the average user that joins your subscriptions service stays for a year and a half (18 months), then you can calculate the average total revenue of a new user by just adding up the cost of a monthly subscription by the number of months they stay a customer.

Let's take the example of Netflix and say that you charge a user $15 a month, and in your marketing, you on average spend a cost to acquire a customer of $20.

Total Revenue	Month 1	Month 2	Month 3	Month 4
	$15	$30	$45	$60

CLV Example

You can see that if you just look at the first month that you actually lost money, since you spent $20 on marketing but only had a revenue of $15. However, after 4 months, you made a total of $60 from that customer and after one year, you'll make $180, so that $20 marketing cost, doesn't look so bad anymore.

Calculating CLV

The CLV (customer lifetime value), is calculated by looking at the total amount of revenue expected to be collected from a customer as long as they are a customer (which is the total amount of revenue from all of their expected purchases).

There are a number of ways to calculate this depending on your business model. However, I found the easiest way is to use to first calculate the average revenue per customer per month (which you would calculate by taking adding the total revenue per customer and dividing it by how many months the customer was with you) and then multiply that by the length of time you want to calculate for (for example 12 months for one year or 24 months for 2 years)

For example, if you the average revenue per customer per month is $100, the CLV (Average Revenue per user or ARPU) for one year would be $1,200 and for 2 years would be $2,400 (the length of time you would take depends on your business).

Churn and profitability

The above way of calculating your CLV is known as your Gross CLV (since you don't take into account profitability, just revenue). If you want to look at your final or Net CLV, then you also have to look at 1) The profit margin for each customer and 2) The average customer **churn** (the percentage of customers that unsubscribe or stop being customers anymore).

The way that you calculate your Net CLV, is similar to how you calculate it above (by taking the average revenue per customer), with the addition of:

Net CLV = ARPU (Average Revenue Per User Per Month) X

Gross Margin per customer (percentage of profit after you subtract all costs, including marketing and operations costs) /

Monthly Churn Rate (percentage of users that cancel or are no longer customers)

For example, if we see that the average revenue per user per month is $100, our gross margins are 40% and our monthly churn rate is 5%, then our Final Net CLV = $100*0.4 / 0.05

= $800

Cohorts

If we assume that we know the average amount of time a user will stay a customer on an overall basis, it's also important to look at different profiles of customers both in terms of how long they stay a customer, their CAC and their CLV. This can be done on a month by month basis (do new customers in January of this year stay longer as customers than new customers in February), or on a demographic basis (do males stay customers longer than females). This study is known as **cohort analysis.**

Non-Subscription

In the case of a subscription business, this is very straightforward, since you know how much to expect in revenue from a customer every month. However, in cases where it's not straightforward, such as an eCommerce store for example where you are not sure how many times a user would buy over their lifetime (for example, they could buy once a year, twice a year or more), you have to look at your historical data and see.

Strategy 2: The 20% approach

If you don't have recurring revenue, or you are unsure if you will, then the next strategy you could implement is one where you make sure that you are profitable from the first transaction. This is harder to achieve, as you need to have your budget be significantly less than your revenue. This is known as the Cost Revenue Ratio, or CRR. It is calculated by taking your costs and dividing them by your revenue. So for example, if you are spending 100 and your revenue is 1000, then your CRR will be: 10/100 or 10%. A good CRR depends on the type of business that you're running and your other costs, but from what I've seen a good rule of thumb is to try to have the number be below 20% (since that's the average marketing budget for most startups and Fortune 500 companies I've come across). Your number may be higher or lower, but if you're unsure, 20% is where I would start as a general benchmark.

Tied in with CRR is the CPA (the cost per acquisition), which is looking at the maximum cost that you're willing to spend per order you receive. This number, like the CRR should have a hard percentage ratio that you never go over. The only difference is that it's on a per transaction basis and not on an overall budget basis.

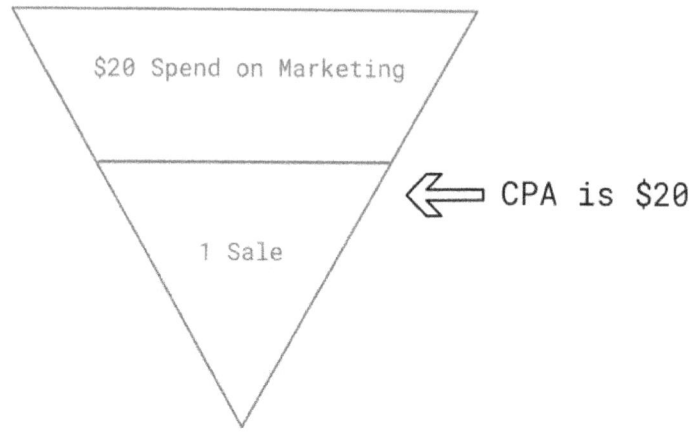

Simple CPA Example

If you have this be your strategy then all you have to do is make sure that you keep the high-level CPA in mind, as well as your CPA on a per channel and per campaign basis. Using this approach, it is very important that you look at all channels holistically and take the multi-channel funnel approach.

For example, it's possible that you have a CPA of $1 on SEO (maybe you're paying for some SEO tools), but your CPA on Display ads is $10. If your target CPA is $7 and the average CPA is $5, then you achieved your target, even though some channels are over your CPA limit.

Example, your Target CPA is $7

Channel	CPA
SEO	$1
Display	$10
Average CPA	$5

Overall CPA Example

Strategy 3: The Inbound Approach

This approach focused more on the free organic ways to build traffic and takes a longer-term approach to marketing and profitability through the following strategies (some of which were outlined in previous chapters).

Focusing on long tail

When you want to focus on getting traffic, it can be hard to stand out in the noise of your competitors. There could be thousands of other websites in the category your business is in. So how do you stand out? The answer is to focus on the long tail (as outlined in Chapter 6).

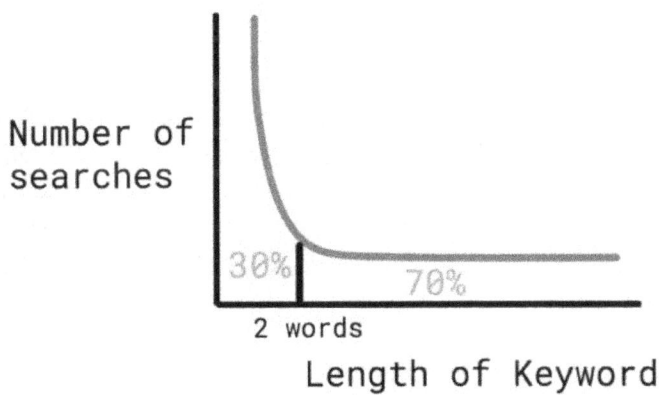

Long Tail

The macro trend in the digital world is there are going to be a few very large players in every industry (Amazon, Google etc.), and a lot of players on the long tail or in individual niches. Therefore, you typically have 2 options when it comes to long term marketing. Either you compete for dominance, or you carve out a niche for yourself and focus on getting targeted traffic. To take a practical example, let's say you offer marketing consulting services and most of your clients are software businesses. It is much easier to be 1 on Google and get organic traffic if you target not just the keyword "marketing consulting services", but rather try something more niche that's in line with what you do like "marketing consulting services for software companies in city X".

Educational Content and answering questions

A very powerful way to bring in a lot of organic traffic, is to not focus on your product or service at all, but instead focus on educating users on topics that are directly (or indirectly related to your industry).

I found that the most effective forms of this are:

1) Answering common questions: The easiest way to get organic traffic to your site and eyeballs on what you're doing is to "skate to where the puck is", which in this case means give people what they want and answer questions they are already asking online! For example, if you're selling widgets and the most common questions people have are related to the differences between widget A and widget B, write a content piece that thoroughly answers that question. You may be thinking, "but how do you find the questions people have online"? The easiest ways are:

   a. To look at the bottom of any search result on Google or any other search engine. If you scroll down to the bottom of the page when you do a search, you'll be given the most common related searches people have, many of which are questions.
   b. Use keywords search traffic data (such as Google Ads Keyword Planner or Google Trends)

c. Use a tools that aggregates all of the questions people ask online (a current popular one is: answerthepublic.com).

2) Deep Diving: Another area in which you can get a lot of organic traffic to your site, is by doing deep dives into various topics. Most content online is very shallow (most web pages according to Google have between 250- 300 words on them). If you write very in-depth content pieces around something in your niche (at least 5,000 words or more), it will skyrocket you to the top of most search results for that topic, since if you are providing useful content you'll have 10 times the information that the sites you're competing with have (taking for granted that you're posting something useful that people want to read). Examples of this could be ultimate guides, in-depth analysis, opinion pieces etc.

3) Fresh Content & Trends: One of the most shocking things that Google has confirmed from their data is that more than 15% of all searches every single day on the web have never been done before! That means that every day 15% of your organic traffic could (in theory) come from brand new keywords that no one in the history of the internet has ever searched for. The final way I recommend to rank for educational content is to always be on the cutting edge. If you constantly update your audience on the latest trends and changes in your industry, you'll get more interest from your audience, and also search engine algorithms will take notice and you'll start ranking for new keywords before your competitors have a chance.

Educational Funnel

Here is an example of what an educational funnel would look like.

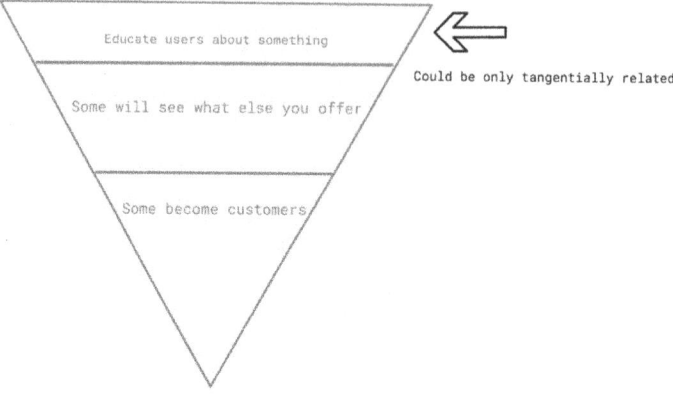

Educational Funnel

For example, if I was running an app to allow you to talk to directly to doctors, I would think about educational content I could create (in the form of videos, blogs or podcasts, etc.) where I could educate the public about either something generic like health tips, or something more directly related to my app like interviewing the doctors on my platform, or creating a free guide on how best to diagnose a medical issue over the phone.

Moving Down the Education Funnel

When it comes to the educational funnel, the idea is that you start off by educating your target audience about something that you offer. That then builds up a following for you as people start seeing you as a **thought leader** in the field. Once you are seen as someone that is an authority figure in a field, it makes it much easier for you to then push people down the funnel to either a soft conversion (having them sign up to your mailing list, following you on social media etc.), and eventually buying from you.

Building your community

Another area you could focus on is building your own community. Human beings are social animals, and we thrive in settings where we can connect with like-minded individuals (our tribes). How this can benefit your digital marketing efforts in the digital world is by having a channel that your grow that provides a sustainable audience for your business. The source of the community could be:

- **Social media channels**: It doesn't have to be all of them, but you could build an audience on a couple of channels where your audience congregates and build your community that way. You could even become an "influencer" if you build a large enough audience. I found that (besides being a fashion or beauty influencer), the easiest way for most businesses to become influential is to focus on posting educational content related to their industry (as mentioned in the previous example).

- **Forum**: This is one of the oldest ways to build a community. A forum is just a message board where people can have discussions and answer questions. Forums have been around since the 90's, and they are still going strong. You could have a self-hosted forum, where you build your own audience, or build a forum as a niche on someone else's platform (for example reddit).

- **Chat Groups**: This is currently the hippest way to build a community. By creating a group on a chat platform, it allows for multiple people to community at the same time, and could take the form of synchronous (where users can chat live, like Slack Discord etc.) or asynchronous chat (like Facebook groups).

- **Email**: Email is the most stable and robust way to grow an audience. Email has been around for decades, and will most likely be around for decades more, plus you have full control over your list, so building an email database is the best way to build an audience.

Strategy 4: The Hybrid Approach

Moving Between Channels

A final parting strategy I want to leave you with is that you'll often times have to mix and match different techniques mentioned here by focusing on different areas depending on your current objectives. Going back to the first chapter, I mentioned how there are 4 main categories of channels.

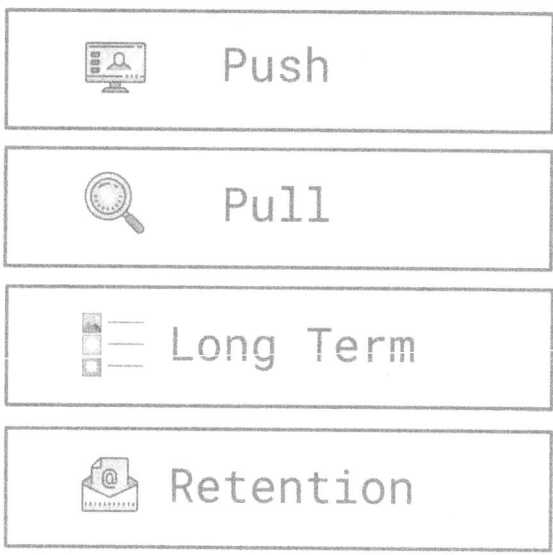

4 Marketing Levels

At different stages of your business you'll find that your focus will also shift. For example, if you are getting no traffic at all and you want to quickly validate your idea, then you'll need to focus on push and pull marketing. If you want to focus on a longer-term approach, and don't have much money to spend, then you'll have to focus on long term and retention marketing. If you're in a growth stage, then you might just focus on all channels at the same time, to maximize your growth, while maintaining profitability across the board.

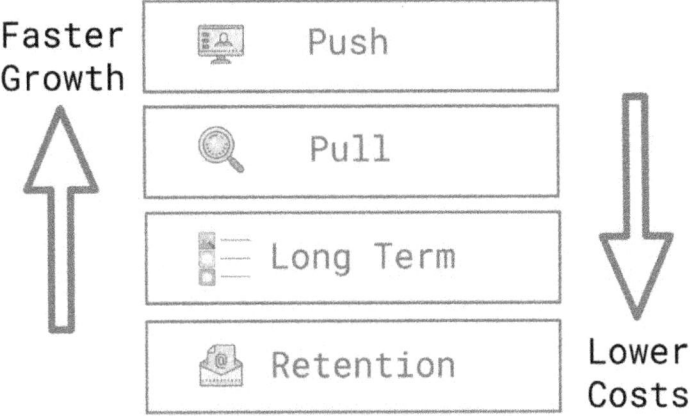

Up and Down

It all depends on what your current goals are.

Action Plan

1. Choose one of the 4 strategies (or a combination of them) to try out for your business

2. Keep optimizing and iterating based on what gets you the most profit.

Conclusion - Now what do I do?

So, what do you do now? You take action! The whole point of this book is to show you the ways in which I recommend you take action towards implementing a successful digital marketing strategy. Whatever your approach, if you follow the principles laid out in this book, I'm sure that you'll be well on your way to building a successful digital marketing strategy.

You can keep learning about digital marketing (and I recommend you do, to stay up-to-date on changes that may happen in the field), however if you don't get your hands dirty and start implementing the strategies laid out in this book, it will be very hard to apply them to your business, and your knowledge will stay theoretical. That's why I recommend that if you want to get serious about using the techniques outlined in this book, start with the action plan items mentioned at the end of each chapter.

My checklist for you, is to do the following in order (summarized from the action points at the end of each chapter):

1. Signup for a tracking platform (I recommend Google Analytics) and install it on your website.
2. Choose at least 2 performance goals that are important for your business (sales, leads, newsletter signups etc.)
3. Track those performance goals either through destination URL's or events (see tools).
4. Setup eCommerce tracking if you have an eCommerce website (see tools)
5. Track the performance of your goals from Google Analytics
6. Install a tag manager (like Google Tag Manager)

7. Install the pixels for any ad platforms you are using (Facebook, Google etc.)
8. Define your profitable CPA number.
9. If you also care about leads for your business, also define your profitable CPL number
10. If your business is one where customers will buy multiple times, define what a profitable CAC number will be.
11. Decide if you want short term gains that you'll have to pay for or if you'd like to focus on long term gains for lower costs
12. Build Your Customer Persona. How would you describe who the people you're targeting are?
13. How will you reach them? Define the kinds of:

   a. Interests and things they dislike
   b. What websites or apps they use
   c. What do they search for online?
   d. Choose the generic and brand keywords you want to target with your ads (including long tail keywords)

14. Start running your first campaigns for Push marketing and Pull marketing
15. SEO, check the technical issues listed in this chapter for your website.
16. SEO, choose the keywords that you want to start targeting for your website, and start adding them to your pages (this needs to be done on each of your top pages)
17. SEO, start looking for link building opportunities with the methods mentioned.
18. Start building content on your website (start a blog if you can), that answers people's questions in your industry
19. Social Media, come up with your tone of voice and the types of content you'd like to start sharing
20. Email, sign up for some email service and start collecting emails.

21. Think of a lead magnet you can give away to people in exchange for their email address
22. Start tracking your Conversion rate on an overall, per goal and per channel basis
23. Start tracking your CPA on an overall, per goal and per channel basis
24. Track your initial ROAS for overall Revenue and Cost
25. Make sure to track your marketing budget against your margins and profits including your multichannel attribution
26. Define your initial marketing budget (starting on a monthly basis)
27. Optimize your campaigns at each of the three levels of the digital ad funnel
28. Once you launch your campaigns, choose your optimization strategy (best CPA, more sales or more leads)
29. Learn to reach your optimal spend level and avoid budget plateauing by frequently changing your ads (at least once a month) and optimizing your bids and budgets.
30. If your marketing is not working, use one of the methods outlined in this chapter, which include changing your: Targeting, Ads, Bids / Budgets, Softer Conversions, Landing Page, and Price
31. Choose one of the 4 strategies: Long term CLM, 20%, Inbound, Hybrid Approach or a combination of them to try out on your business.
32. Keep optimizing and iterating based on what gets you the most profit.

Thanks for reaching the end of this book. If you have any questions about anything covered, or would just like to say hi, feel free to send me an email at: ahmadabugosh@gmail.com

For a constantly updated list of the tools I use, along with guides on how to use them, check out: http://tools.timelessdigitalmarketing.com

May your success be as timeless as the principles in this book!

Glossary of terms

This book covers a lot of ground. If you ever get lost by a word used in the book, you can refer to the glossary of terms below to get back on track (sorted in alphabetical order).

Ads: Any form of promotion that is shown to users. Usually this will be some text, and in certain channels may be accompanied with videos and images.

Ad blocker: A piece of software you can activate on your browser or phone that blocks ads from appearing to you. It is not 100% effective as it tries to bypass how ads are inserted, and ad platforms always try to block them.

Ad network: A platform that connects advertisers to content creators, so advertisers can easily find places to show their ads, and content creators can make money from showing ads on their platform.

Affiliates: The people, websites or apps that promote your products, usually as part of an affiliate program (they get paid based on commissions).

Affiliate Marketing: Marketing that is done based on other people promoting your product and being paid on commission. This usually takes the form of bloggers, influencers or other content creators that post a special link and get paid for every referral.

ASO (App Store Optimization): The term used for marketing that is done to make mobile apps appear higher in search engine results organically (without having to pay). This is mainly done by optimizing content for Android and iOS (the Play Store and App store respectively). These techniques are similar in nature to how SEO is done.

Audiences (targeting): These are the people you target with your marketing. This could be based on demographics, behaviour, interests, or contact details (mainly their emails and phone numbers).

Automated emails: Any email that is sent automatically. All automated emails have two sections 1) A Trigger (what causes the email to be sent) and 2) The email itself.

Average Session Duration: The amount of time that a user spends on your website on average.

Awareness Goals: Any goal that you track where the objective is not to get more sales or leads, but instead raise awareness for a product or service.

Brand Advocates: A brand advocate is another word for an affiliate.

Bounce Rate: The percentage ratio of bounces over sessions. The formula for this is Bounces / Sessions.

Bounces: The number of times a user leaves your site without going to another page on your website.

Budget: The amount of money you are willing to spend for marketing. This could be overall for all marketing, or specific to a channel, or campaign.

Cohort A grouping of customers, which in marketing is usually done on a month basis (for example, all of the customers in August).

Checkout / Goal Flow: The sequence of steps a user takes when they buy a product. For example, cart, checkout, and thank you page.

Click: The number of times an ad is clicked on by a user. In theory, this number should be the same as the number of sessions / visits.

Content Marketing: Marketing done through developing content that people find organically (for free) via search engines and social media.

Content (targeting): These are the websites or apps where your ads show up when you do marketing

CAC Cost per acquisition of a customer. This is similar to CPA in that it measures the cost needed to acquire a transaction. However, with CAC you're measuring if someone becomes a customer instead of just a one-time transaction. Usually this means you're expecting the customer to make more than one, or recurring transactions.

CLV Customer Lifetime Value. The monetary value (revenue) a customer is worth to you, over the lifetime that they are a customer.

Conversions: A completed goal, that usually has a monetary value associated with it.

CPA: Cost per acquisition. The amount you'll be expected to pay, to receive an acquisition (this is a goal that you define)

CPC: Cost per click. This is the amount that you pay to get one click on your ad.

CPE Cost per engagement. The amount you pay for some engagement with your ad (could be a comment, hover etc.). This is calculated differently on every platform.

CPM: Cost per milli or Cost per thousand impressions. This is the amount of money you pay to have your ad get 1,000 impressions (regardless of clicks or engagement).

CPV Cost per video view. The amount that you pay whenever a video view is recorded. This is calculated differently on every platform

Creatives: Any graphics, images, or videos used as ads

Destination URL Goals: A goal that is defined based on an action taken by a user that cases the page or screen to change. For example, if a user submits a form and are taking to a thank you page / screen. This is the easiest form of goal tracking, as it does not require any additional codes to be installed (unlike event tracking).

Digital Marketing: Any form of marketing or promoting a product or service using online or digital means.

Dimensions: An attribution of data used in reporting. Dimensions are qualitative data type (not numbers or percentages). For example, Country, Page, and Channel.

Direct Response Marketing: Same definition as performance marketing.

Drip campaigns: A form of automated email campaigns in which content is spread across multiple emails (dripped out slowly) to email subscribers.

Email Marketing: Marketing that is done via email. This is usually done through special software that lets you send emails in bulk.

Email Trigger: The condition under which an automated email is sent. This can be 1) Time based: On a certain time or date 2) Activity Based: If a user interacts with a previous email 3) Website Based: If a user does some action on the website or app or 4) Audience based: If a user meets certain conditions (for example, it's their birthday).

Email Sequence: A series of automated emails sent to a user.

Engagement: Any interaction with your ad that is not a click or a form submission is an ad engagement. For example, playing a video, liking or commenting on a post.

Event Goals: A goal defined based on a completed event.

Events: An action that is taken on a website or app, that does not cause the page or screen to change (also known as an in-page action). An example of this is a form submission that keeps the user on the same page. Tracking events usually require additional custom code to be added onto your website / app.

Exit Page: The opposite of a landing page, an exit page is the last page a user goes on before a user leaves your site.

Floodlight pixel: Another name for a tag manager.

Frequency: The amount of time your ad gets seen by a single user.

Frequency Cap: A cap that you put on your ad so it doesn't get seen more than this amount over a certain period (for example, 5 times per day).

Goals: Any desirable action you want to track on your website.

Growth Hacking: A generic term that generally means using low cost "hacks" or techniques to grow your business in a non-traditional way. These hacks can work well, but they change so often that they may be unsustainable.

Impression: Every time an ad is loaded on the app or screen of the user, an impression is counted.

Inbound Marketing: Same meaning as "Content Marketing"

Influencer Marketing: The form of marketing that involves someone with a lot of followers on a social media channel (Instagram, YouTube etc.) get paid for promoting a product or service. There is no hard minimum number of followers to be considered an influencer, but people with not that many followers (less than 10,000 or so) are usually called **Microinfluencers**.

Landing Page: This is the starting page a user lands on when they first come to your website. It is also a term used in the marketing community for a page used for marketing purposes (since people first land there from marketing efforts).

Long term marketing: Marketing done without paying money or at a low cost. The trade-off is that you have to spend time in generating long term interest.

Lookalike audiences: An auto generated audience you can use in your ad, that finds people that are similar to your existing audience.

Matched audiences: An audience that is defined on an ad platform, when you upload customer data (like emails and phone numbers), which allows you to target your existing customers through ads.

Metrics: A value that is calculated in relation to a dimension. Metrics are quantitative data types (numbers or percentages). Examples are: Conversion Rate, Average Order Value, Number of Orders etc.

Newsletter: A standard email that is sent out to your email list.

Online Marketing: Another word for Digital Marketing.

Pageview / Hit / Screenview: Anytime a new page or a screen loads on a website or app.

Paid social media: Ads run on social media channels where you pay to have your ad be promoted. These could be promoted posts, videos, lead forms or other types of ads.

Programmatic ads: Any ads that are automatically optimized and adjusted. This is usually done through an agency where software is used and is a lot more expensive than running ads on your own.

Publishers: The websites or apps where a promoted ad shows up on.

Organic social media: Social media posting done without paying money.

Page: A view within your website.

Performance Goals: Any goal that you track where the objective is directly tied to business revenue (either as leads or sales).

Performance Marketing: Marketing done in a scientific systematized way where you measure the results of your how people respond to your efforts based on your ROI (return on investment).

Pixels: A piece of code put on your website or app used for marketing tracking purposes.

Pull Marketing: Meeting people halfway by pulling them onto your product / server, after they show initial interest (usually through a search). Online this is by showing ads on search engines like Google.

Push Marketing: Pushing your ad out in front of people, before they show any interest in you. Online this is images or videos ads.

Reach: The total potential number of people that could see your ad, if your budget was unlimited.

Referral: Any traffic, lead or sale sent to you by someone else (through their social media, website or app).

Remarketing: Marketing done to people that previously visited your site / app **Retargeting:** Targeting people that previously visited your site / app. For all intents and purposes, it has the same meaning as Remarketing.

ROI (Return on Investment): An indication of how well your marketing efforts are doing. This measures the revenue versus the cost to see how profitable you are. The usual formula is Revenue / Cost (as a percentage).

Screen: A view within your app. It is similar to a page, but for mobile apps.

SERP: Stands for Search Engine Results page. This is the page that you see in Google (or any other search engine) when you search for any word.

SEA (Search Engine Advertising): The term used exclusively for marketing done through paid search engine ads.

SEM (Search Engine Marketing): The term used to describe all marketing done on search engines (like Google). This often times is used to describe only the paid marketing done, but the term could mean both paid and unpaid search engine marketing.

Session: Every time a user goes to (visits) a website, it counts as a session.

SEO (Search Engine Optimization): The term used for marketing that is done to make your website appear higher in search engine results organically (without having to pay for ads).

Session Window: The time period set by which the session or visit will time out if there is no activity on the page or screen by the user. For most websites or apps this is set to 30 minutes by default, but it can be changed if needed. After this amount of time of inactivity, a new session will be registered.

Session: Every time a user going to a website or app over a period of time. This is counted on a time basis and if there is no activity by the user after a certain period of time (For example, 30 minutes of no activity) then the session is ended.

SMO (Social Media Optimization): The term used for marketing that is done to make social media profiles and content appear higher in search engine results organically (without having to pay).

Stories: A short video or image that is shown to a user for 24 hours. This trend started with Snapchat, and then was further popularized by Instagram.

Subscribers: The people that opted in (chose) to be on your email list.

Tag manager: A tool you can install on your website / app that makes it easy to add multiple tracking codes on your website, without touching your code.

Tagged URL: A URL that has tracking implemented on it.

Targeting: How you are filtering where your ads show up. There are two main types of targeting: a) Content or b) Audiences.

Tracking code: Same definition as pixel (A piece of code put on your website or app used for marketing tracking purposes).

Tracking URL: A URL or deep link (link to an app), that adds special information to your traffic, which allows you to track its marketing source.

Traffic: The number of visits or sessions that your app or website gets.

Transactional emails: A form of automated email that is sent out once a user completes a goal or transaction.

Transactions: Same definition as a conversion, but usually used in eCommerce websites (sites where you sell something).

User: A person (human) that visited your website / app.

Users: The number of people who visited your website. This is calculated on a browser basis (so if the same user goes on your website on two different browsers or devices it will count multiple users), The only way to avoid this is to have users log in.

UTM parameter: Specific to Google Analytics, this is a URL that is tagged with Google's tracking URL.

Viewable Impression: The number of times an impression is counted, but only if that ad is someone directly on the screen of the user (and not at the bottom of the page for example)

Visit: Same definition as session.

Workflows: The series of steps or sequence of emails sent in a drip campaign

Appendix of Tools

In this book, I didn't talk that much about tools, because they change so often. However, as I mentioned earlier, for a constantly updated list of the tools I use, along with guides on how to use them, check out: [http://tools.timelessdigitalmarketing.com][1]

[1]: http://tools.timelessdigitalmarketing.com

CPSIA information can be obtained
at www.ICGtesting.com
Printed in the USA
LVHW111651250421
685526LV00006B/1045